SEX CRIMINALS

FOURGY

MATT FRACTION
CHIP ZDARSKY

ELIZABETH BREITWEISER
COLORS (CHAPTER 17)

THOMAS K
EDITING

DREW GILL
PRODUCTION

LAUREN SANKOVITCH
MANAGING EDITOR

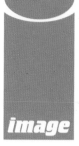

IMAGE COMICS, INC.
Robert Kirkman—Chief Operating Officer
Erik Larsen—Chief Financial Officer
Todd McFarlane—President
Marc Silvestri—Chief Executive Officer
Jim Valentino—Vice President

Eric Stephenson—Publisher
Corey Murphy—Director of Sales
Jeff Boison—Director of Publishing Planning & Book Trade Sales
Chris Ross—Director of Digital Sales
Jeff Stang—Director of Specialty Sales
Kat Salazar—Director of PR & Marketing
Branwyn Bigglestone—Controller
Kat Dugan—Senior Accounting Manager
Sue Korpela—Accounting & HR Manager
Drew Gill—Art Director
Heather Doornink—Production Director
Leigh Thomas—Print Manager
Tricia Ramos—Traffic Manager
Briah Skelly—Publicist
Aly Hoffman—Events & Conventions Coordinator
Sasha Head—Sales & Marketing Production Designer
David Brothers—Branding Manager
Melissa Gifford—Content Manager
Drew Fitzgerald—Publicity Assistant
Vincent Kukua—Production Artist
Erika Schnatz—Production Artist
Ryan Brewer—Production Artist
Shanna Matuszak—Production Artist
Carey Hall—Production Artist
Esther Kim—Direct Market Sales Representative
Emilio Bautista—Digital Sales Representative
Leanna Caunter—Accounting Analyst
Chloe Ramos-Peterson—Library Market Sales Representative
Maria Eizik—Administrative Assistant
IMAGECOMICS.COM

For Chip,
By the time you read this
I'll be gone
You son of a bitch

MATT

For Chip,
You're a self-made man
And that's what I respect about you.
Also, your undying patience with others.
Also, your nice penis.

CHIP

16
GOALS

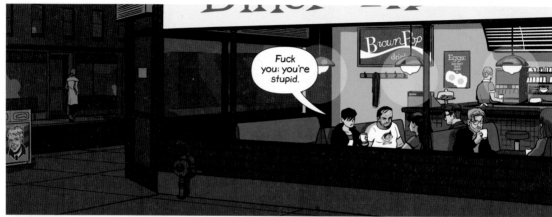

Fuck you; you're stupid.

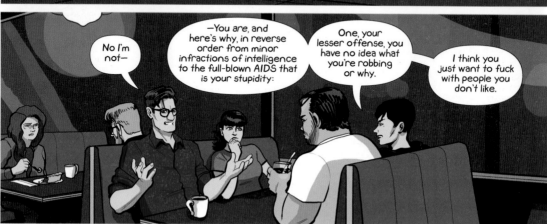

No I'm not—

—You *are*, and here's why, in reverse order from minor infractions of intelligence to the full-blown AIDS that is your stupidity:

One, your lesser offense, you have no idea what you're robbing or why.

I think you just want to fuck with people you don't like.

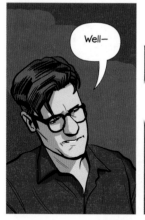

Well—

—Shut up, because, two, you're fucking stupid because everything you decide to do is hot blooded and personal.

You're talking about breaking real goddamn laws because this she-demon's fucking with you.

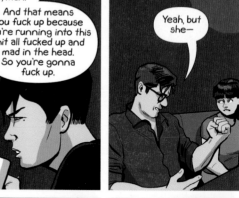

She's got you *riled*, man.

And that means you fuck up because you're running into this shit all fucked up and mad in the head. So you're gonna fuck up.

Yeah, but she—

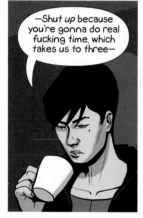

—Shut *up* because you're gonna do real fucking time, which takes us to three—

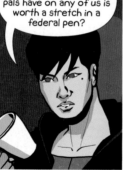

—The fuck makes you think anything Myrtle Spurge and her pals have on any of us is worth a stretch in a federal pen?

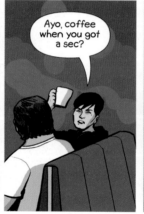

Ayo, coffee when you got a sec?

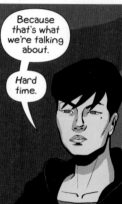

Because that's what we're talking about.

Hard time.

Here's the thing—We know what she's done, and I promise all y'all crackers I know more about her than you—
What can you *prove* she's done?
She—they—
—I'm going to do that thing where I answer my own question, sweetie.
You can't prove she's done a goddamn thing.
You might not even realize it right now, but I promise you—legally there's not only no case here, there's no cause.
And that is entirely by her design.
She broke into my office! She stole Jon's file!
We don't need to tell her—
What? It's true! She committed a crime!
Hahaha!
Oh, shit, son, you're cooked.
I guarantee it, you've got nothing. Here, watch:
She enter forcibly?
I—no.
Did she have cause to be there?
I—she—we—
...Yes.
She wearing gloves, by any chance?

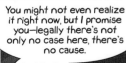

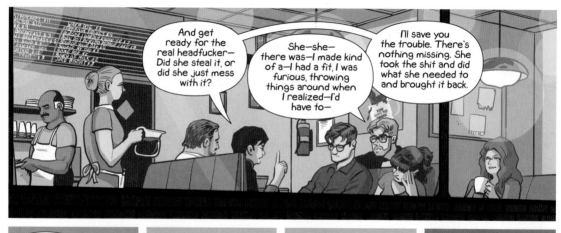

And get ready for the real headfucker—Did she steal it, or did she just mess with it?

She—she—there was—I made kind of a—I had a fit, I was furious, throwing things around when I realized—I'd have to—

I'll save you the trouble. There's nothing missing. She took the shit and did what she needed to and brought it back.

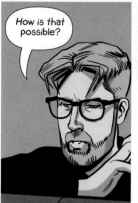

How is that possible?

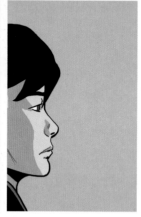

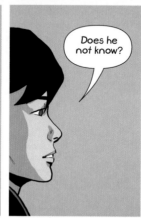

Does he not know?

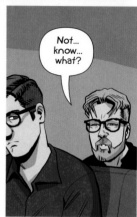

Not... know... what?

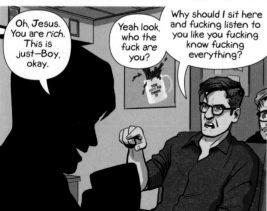

Oh, Jesus. You are *rich.* This is just—Boy, okay.

Yeah look, who the fuck are you? Why should I sit here and fucking listen to you like you fucking know fucking everything?

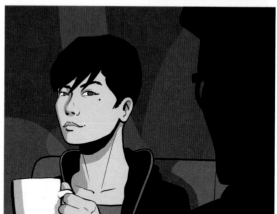

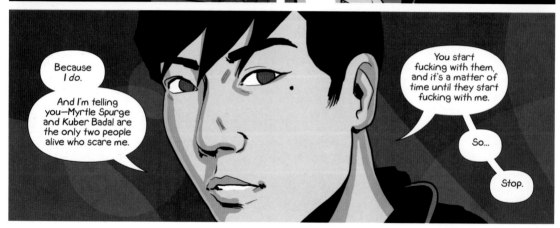

Because I *do.*

And I'm telling you—Myrtle Spurge and Kuber Badal are the only two people alive who scare me.

You start fucking with them, and it's a matter of time until they start fucking with me.

So...

Stop.

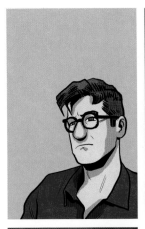

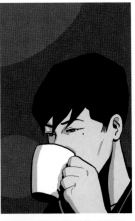

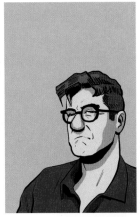

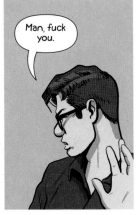
Man, fuck you.

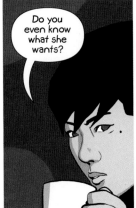
Do you even know what she wants?

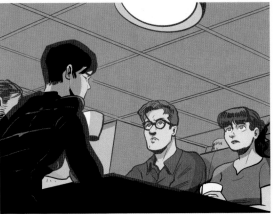

Because I see a guy Kool-Aid Man-ing into federal time, and dragging his friends along with him like a retarded Don Quixote.

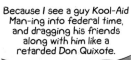
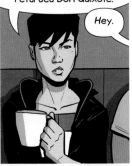
Hey.

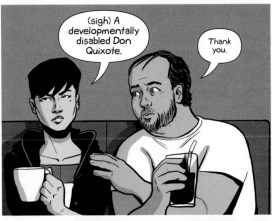
(sigh) A developmentally disabled Don Quixote.

Thank you.

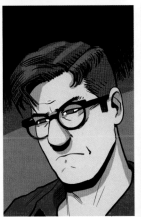

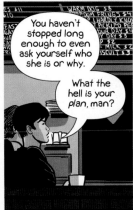
You haven't stopped long enough to even ask yourself who she is or why.

What the hell is your *plan*, man?

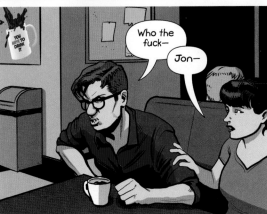
Who the fuck—

Jon—

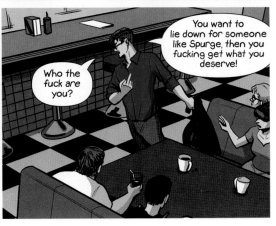
Who the fuck *are* you?

You want to lie down for someone like Spurge, then you fucking get what you deserve!

And you—
You touch me again? *Hit* me again?
I will beat the living *fuck* out you, pal.
No you won't.
DANG!
Nailed it, Dewey.
Fuck you.
...Dr. Kincaid, if you could cover us—
That asshole.
Jon you unbelievable fucking—

reat
—ASSHOLE!
BOOM BOOM CHIC
SEXUAL GARY 4 SEXUAL PRESIDENT 2017
Hey. Jon, hey—
—Man, fuck her.
She's a bitch, right? And that fucking man-mountain of hers—
HEY.
PRODUCTS MARKED UP FOR THE BIG CITY
Don't do that to me.
You.
Don't do that to me.
New claimed wood in stock!
-Old barn door
-Old 4X4 holding up a hoarder's house
-Bunch of toothpicks
-Old floor of a haunted church
...I—
Don't storm out of a, y'know, don't go make a big fucking exit—
Baby—
Fuck you, "baby." I'm not a goddamn lapdog, and I don't come when you snap your fingers.
Really? You too now?
You want to get up and leave, you don't leave me behind to make apologies and scurry after you.
We're a *team*.
And you left me *behind*.
ASSHOLE!

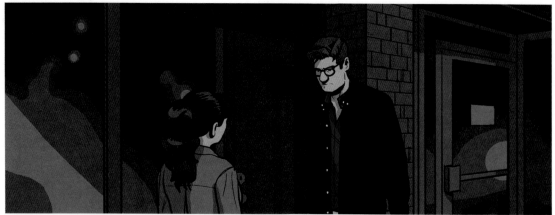

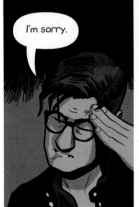

I'm sorry.

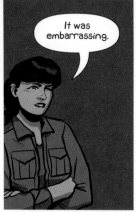

It was embarrassing.

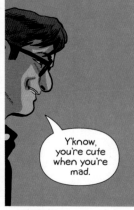

Okay...!

OKAY?!

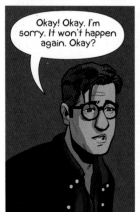

Okay! Okay. I'm sorry. It won't happen again. Okay?

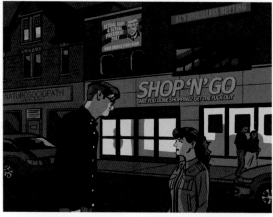

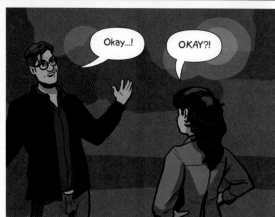

Y'know, you're cute when you're mad.

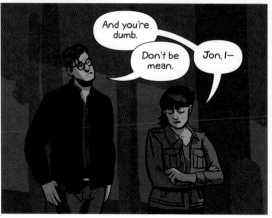

And you're dumb.

Don't be mean.

Jon, I—

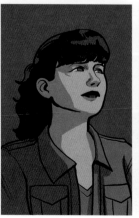

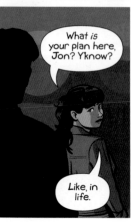

What is your plan here, Jon? Y'know?

Like, in life.

Uh...
We're walking home?
You ever think... bigger picture... than that?
She kinda had a point there at the end. I mean—
What are you doing, Jon? What are we? Doing?
oh shit
don't say I love you again don't say I love you again don't say
Suzie, I...
THURSDAYS!
SEXUAL GARY 4 SEXUAL PRESIDENT
HOPE
HIRST'S ART SUPPLIES
I just want to go to bed.

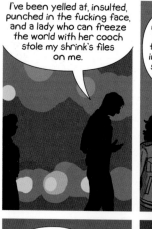

I've been yelled at, insulted, punched in the fucking face, and a lady who can freeze the world with her cooch stole my shrink's files on me.

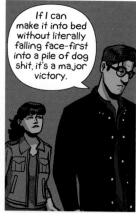

If I can make it into bed without literally falling face-first into a pile of dog shit, it's a major victory.

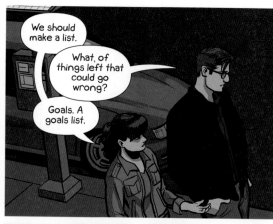

We should make a list.

What, of things left that could go wrong?

Goals. A goals list.

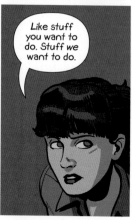

Like stuff you want to do. Stuff we want to do.

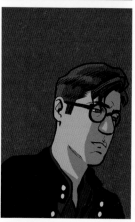

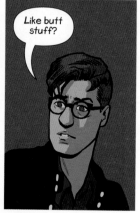

Like butt stuff?

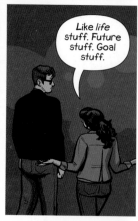

Like life stuff. Future stuff. Goal stuff.

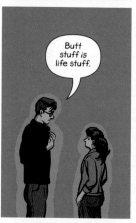

Butt stuff is life stuff.

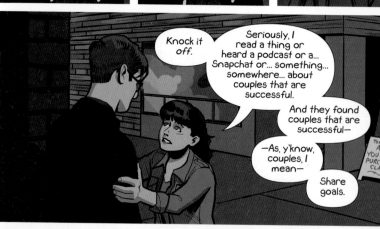

Knock it off.

Seriously, I read a thing or heard a podcast or a... Snapchat or... something... somewhere... about couples that are successful.

And they found couples that are successful—

—As, y'know, couples, I mean—

Share goals.

TONIGHT, ALL YOU CAN PURCHASE CLAMS

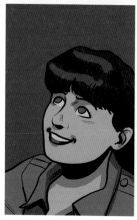

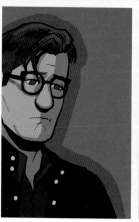

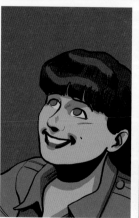

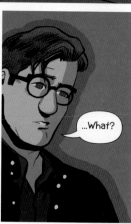

...What?

They all had the same, like, things in general that they wanted.
They wanted to own a home or they wanted to go on a vacation to Israel and buy a Super Mario yarmulke or—
—Butt stuff—
(sigh)
Yes, butt stuff.
Anyway, I know it sounds cheesy and stuff, but maybe we could have that talk and see where we're at.
What?
I don't know how to do this, Suzanne.
You just think of stuff you want, and then *write*—
No, I mean—
I mean *this*.

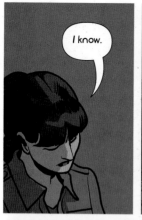

I know.

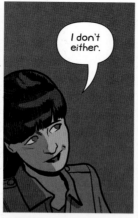

I don't either.

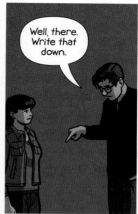

Well, there. Write that down.

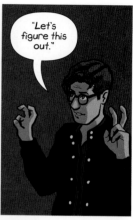

"Let's figure this out."

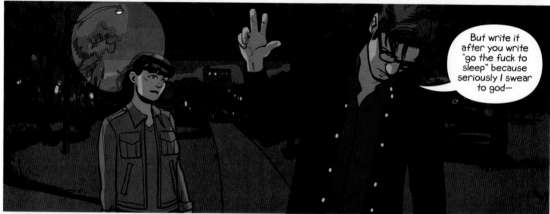

But write it after you write "go the fuck to sleep" because seriously I swear to god—

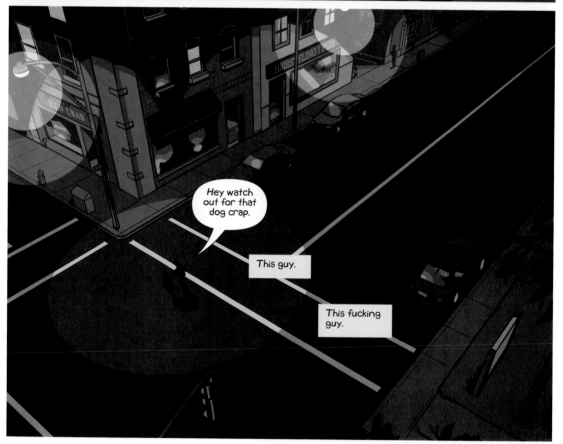

Hey watch out for that dog crap.

This guy.

This fucking guy.

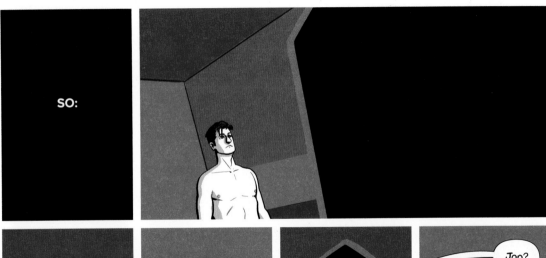

SO:

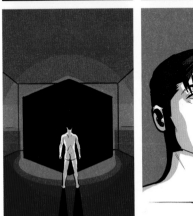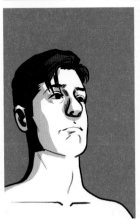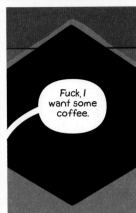

Fuck, I want some coffee.

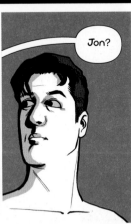

Jon?

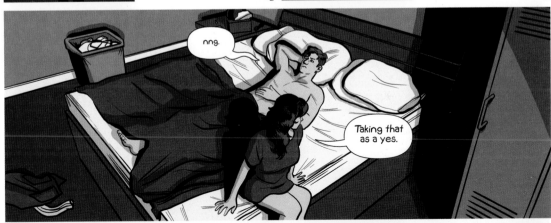

nng.

Taking that as a yes.

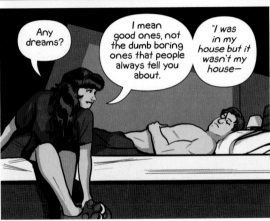

Any dreams?

I mean good ones, not the dumb boring ones that people always tell you about.

"I was in my house but it wasn't my house—"

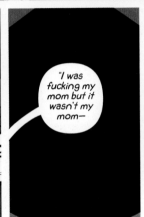

"I was fucking my mom but it wasn't my mom—"

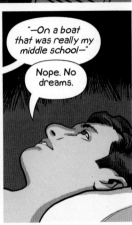

"—On a boat that was really my middle school—"

Nope. No dreams.

We have anything happening today?
TAFT
Think I have rehearsal this afternoon, but—
What's wrong.
Wait what's happening—?
BONE JUICE
We're gonna talk about our goals.
Right?
Remember?
I—
You—
—Fucking *nerd.*
BONE JUICE
But.
My markers.
So... brunch? Dunchfast? That new meal people are eating after second blunch but before you go to sleep?
Because we will *never* get a res at Cloche D'taco this late.
This, Jon.
We're gonna do this, and we're gonna feel dorky and stupid and weird and awkward as we do it, but we're gonna do it.
And look I brought markers.

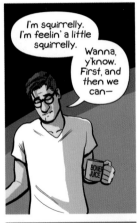

I'm squirrelly. I'm feelin' a little squirrelly.

Wanna, y'know. First, and then we can—

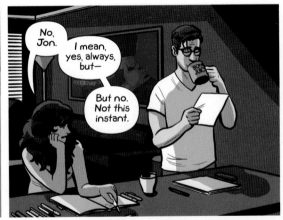

No, Jon.

I mean, yes, always, but—

But no. Not this instant.

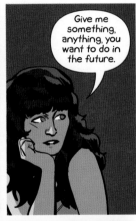

Give me something, anything, you want to do in the future.

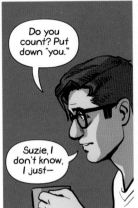

Do you count? Put down "you."

Suzie, I don't know, I just—

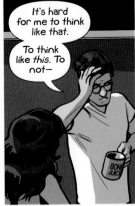

It's hard for me to think like that.

To think like this. To not—

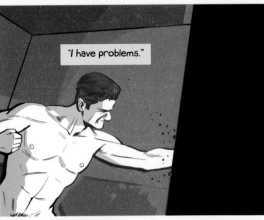

"I have problems."

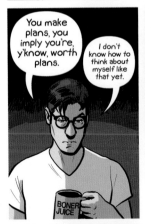

You make plans, you imply you're, y'know, worth plans.

I don't know how to think about myself like that yet.

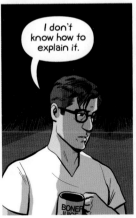

I don't know how to explain it.

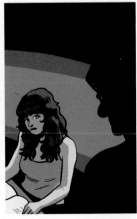

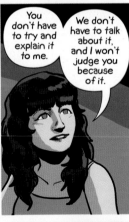

You don't have to try and explain it to me.

We don't have to talk about it, and I won't judge you because of it.

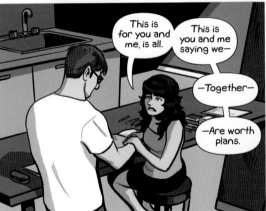

This is for you and me, is all.

This is you and me saying we—

—Together—

—Are worth plans.

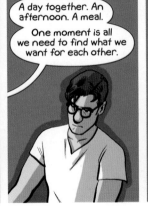

A day together. An afternoon. A meal.

One moment is all we need to find what we want for each other.

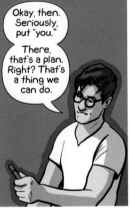

Okay, then. Seriously, put "you."

There, that's a plan. Right? That's a thing we can do.

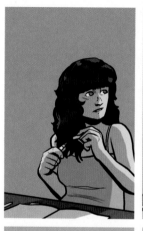

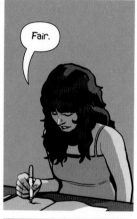
Fair.

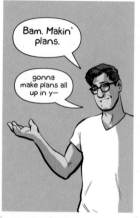
Bam. Makin' plans.

gonna make plans all up in y—

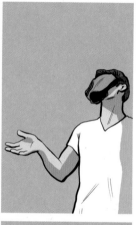

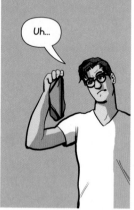
Uh...

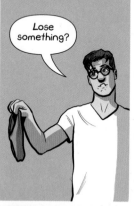
Lose something?

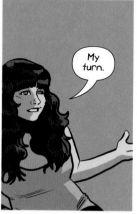
My turn.

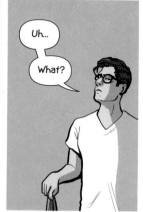
Uh...

What?

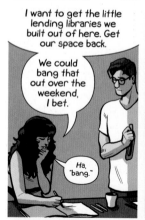
I want to get the little lending libraries we built out of here. Get our space back.

We could bang that out over the weekend, I bet.

Ha, "bang."

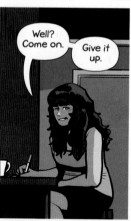
Well? Come on.

Give it up.

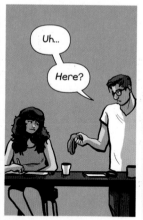
Uh...

Here?

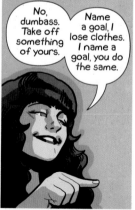
No, dumbass. Take off something of yours.

Name a goal, I lose clothes. I name a goal, you do the same.

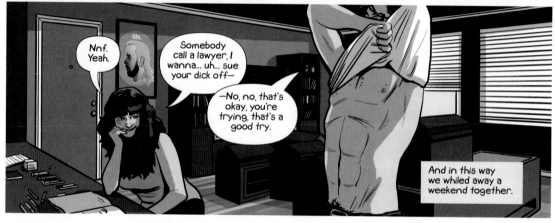
Nnf. Yeah.

Somebody call a lawyer, I wanna... uh... sue your dick off—

—No, no, that's okay, you're trying, that's a good try.

And in this way we whiled away a weekend together.

If you were to ask me what were "the good old days," it's the stuff like this that would come to mind.
Everything was sexy and silly and serious all at the same time.
It was like we were at sea together and had to figure out how to make a boat work.
Wait, what's the difference between a boat and a ship?
Well whatever. We were together and trying to figure out how.
It was okay though.
O'NUTS
We had each other.
I didn't want to push him on his head stuff and he didn't really offer to pull me in, for which I was grateful.
I didn't want to fix him and he didn't want me to try.
All I wanted him to know was that I cared about him and he was worth it.
Even if on some level he didn't think he was worth caring for.

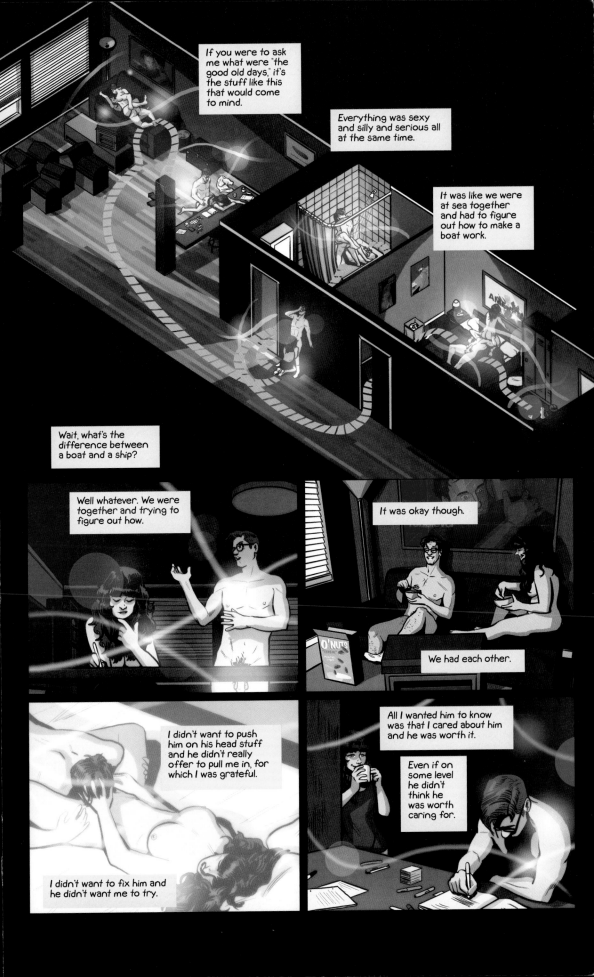

I don't pretend to be a, like, mental health, y'know, expert, or self-care specialist or anything.
All I could do was hold his hand and see if he wanted to come along with me.
And he did.
Well, he didn't come along with me *every* time.
I laughed so hard two drops of pee came out—
—and then we started laughing all over again.
Two against the world with all the lo mein we could eat. Which, it turns out, is a lot.
robolover
We talked. About anything. About everything.
We made great spans of plans and gathered a gaggle of goals. Things for today, tomorrow, next month, next winter, next year.
And we screwed like they were gonna take it away.
After a while it wasn't even about the Quiet anymore. He'd go in, I'd go in, and we'd wait and chase each other all over again.
It was fine.
Everything was going to be fine.
I hate this.
Thanks.

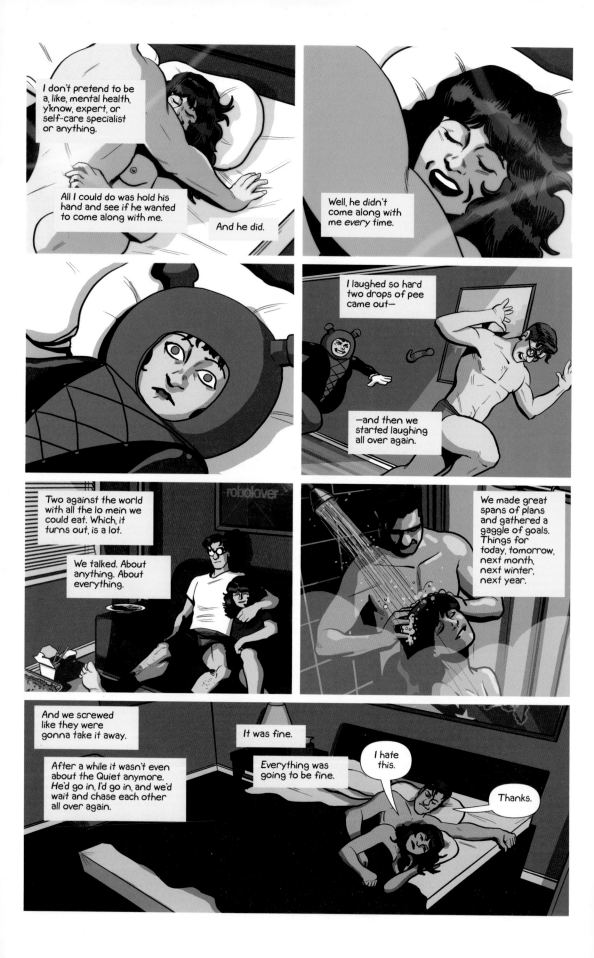

No, I mean—
spooning, okay,
look, it's sweet...
But...
But.
It never lasts.
Something falls asleep, or
you need a drink, or—
—Been together
like six months,
you're just now—
—No, I
know, I'm sorry,
I just...
Just.
Y'know. Full
disclosure?
Sleeping like
this, it never
lasts...
well
fuck me.

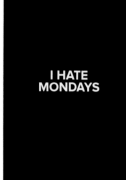

I HATE
MONDAYS

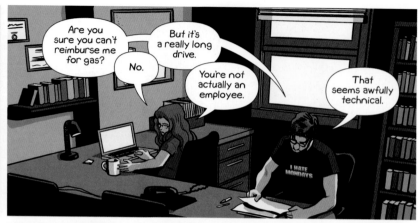

Are you sure you can't reimburse me for gas?

No.

But it's a really long drive.

You're not actually an employee.

That seems awfully technical.

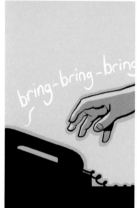

bring-bring-bring

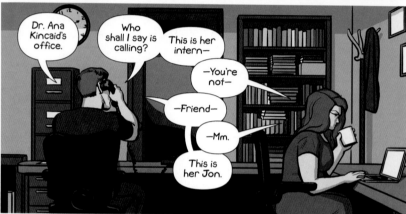

Dr. Ana Kincaid's office.

Who shall I say is calling?

This is her intern—

—You're not—

—Friend—

—Mm.

This is her Jon.

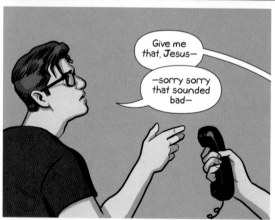

Give me that, Jesus—

—sorry sorry that sounded bad—

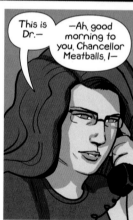

This is Dr.—

—Ah, good morning to you, Chancellor Meatballs, I—

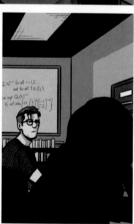

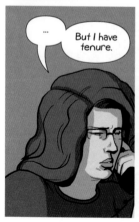

... But I have tenure.

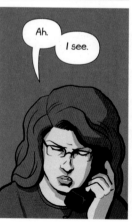

Ah.

I see.

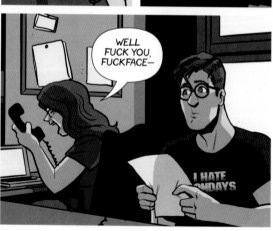

WELL FUCK YOU, FUCKFACE—

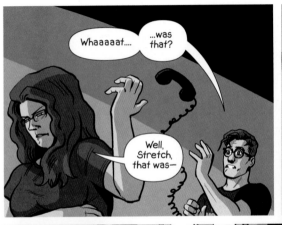

Whaaaaat.... ...was that?

Well, Stretch, that was—

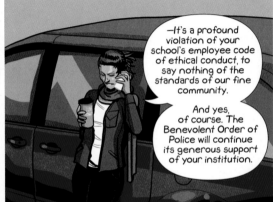

—It's a profound violation of your school's employee code of ethical conduct, to say nothing of the standards of our fine community.

And yes, of course. The Benevolent Order of Police will continue its generous support of your institution.

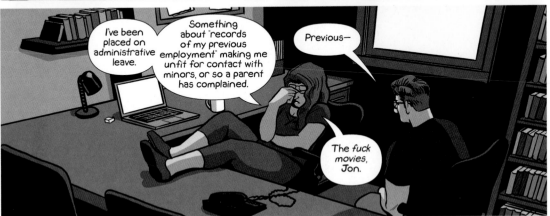

I've been placed on administrative leave.

Something about "records of my previous employment" making me unfit for contact with minors, or so a parent has complained.

Previous—

The *fuck* movies, Jon.

I just—

Doesn't it seem like—

Kegelface.

KEGELFACE.

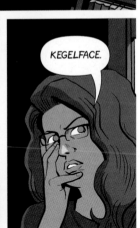

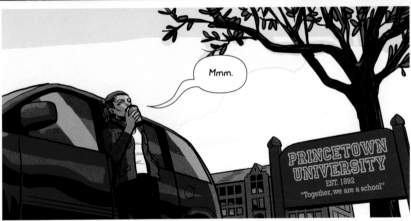

Mmm.

PRINCETOWN UNIVERSITY
EST. 1892
"Together, we are a school"

17 THE SKELL

LAST CHAPTER

AFTER JON AND SUZE WAKE UP

BUT LIKE JUST BEFORE

ANA GETS THE PHONE CALL

WELL NOT JUST

BUT BEFORE THAT BUT

AFTER THE OTHER

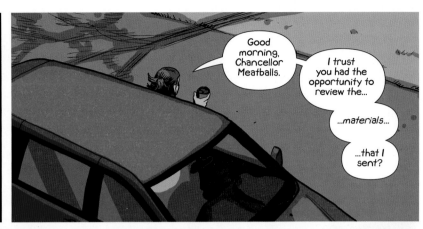

Good morning, Chancellor Meatballs.

I trust you had the opportunity to review the...

...materials...

...that I sent?

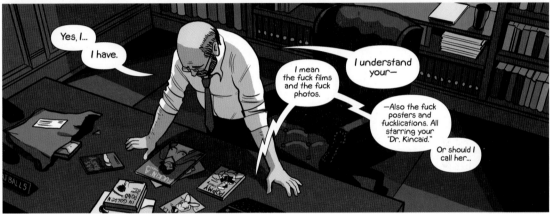

Yes, I...

I have.

I mean the fuck films and the fuck photos.

I understand your—

—Also the fuck posters and fucklications. All starring your "Dr. Kincaid."

Or should I call her...

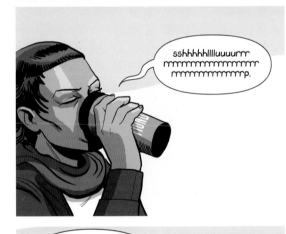

sshhhhhlllluuuurrr rrrrrrrrrrrrrrrr rrrrrrrrrrrrrrrp.

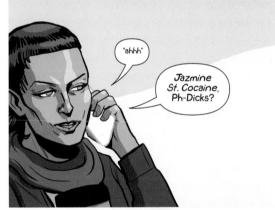

ahhh

Jazmine St. Cocaine, Ph-Dicks?

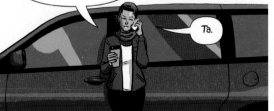

Yes, I agree, immediate termination is the only remedy. It's a profound violation of your school's employee code of ethical conduct, to say nothing of the standards of our fine community.

And yes, of course. The Benevolent Order of Police will continue its generous support of your institution.

Ta.

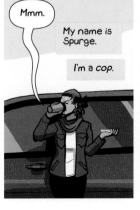

Mmm.

My name is Spurge.

I'm a *cop*.

OH SHIT

SEX CRIMINALs

ED BRUBAKER + SEAN PHILLIPS
MATT + CHIP
+ BETTIE

PART 2:
MYRTLE SPURGE:
SEXUAL COP

Chip 2016
+
Sean
2008

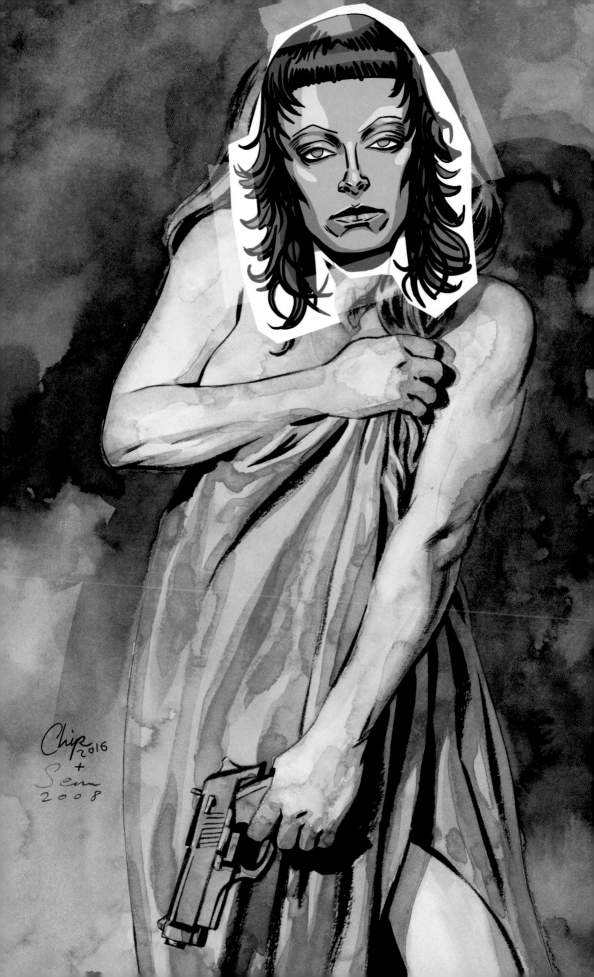

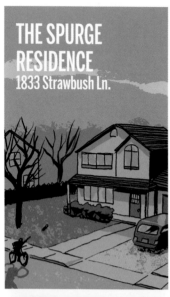

THE SPURGE RESIDENCE
1833 Strawbush Ln.

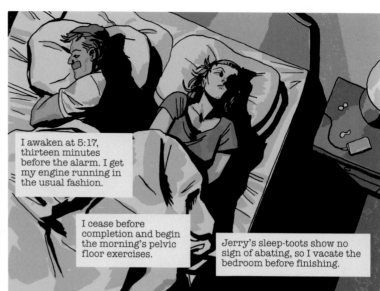

I awaken at 5:17, thirteen minutes before the alarm. I get my engine running in the usual fashion.

I cease before completion and begin the morning's pelvic floor exercises.

Jerry's sleep-toots show no sign of abating, so I vacate the bedroom before finishing.

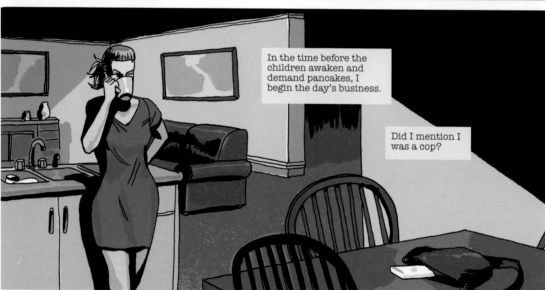

In the time before the children awaken and demand pancakes, I begin the day's business.

Did I mention I was a cop?

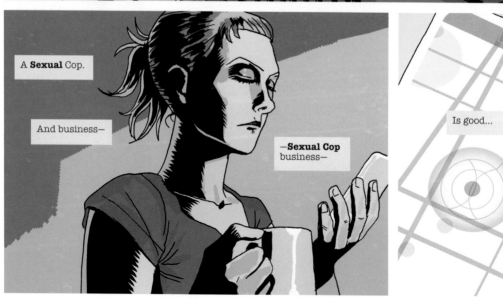

A **Sexual** Cop.

And business—

—**Sexual Cop** business—

Is good...

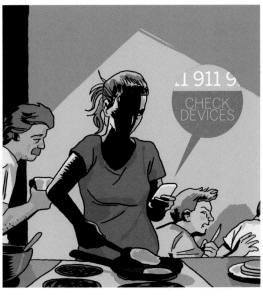

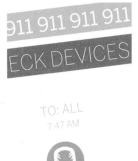

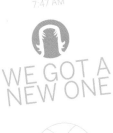

TO: ALL
7:47 AM

WE GOT A
NEW ONE

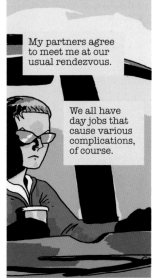

My partners agree to meet me at our usual rendezvous.

We all have day jobs that cause various complications, of course.

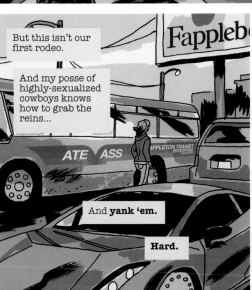

But this isn't our first rodeo.

And my posse of highly-sexualized cowboys knows how to grab the reins...

And **yank 'em.**

Hard.

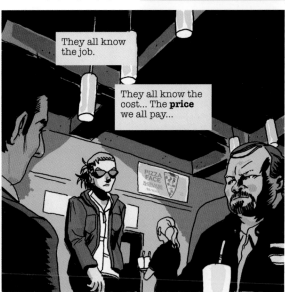

They all know the job.

They all know the cost... The **price** we all pay...

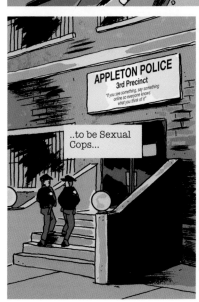

..to be Sexual Cops...

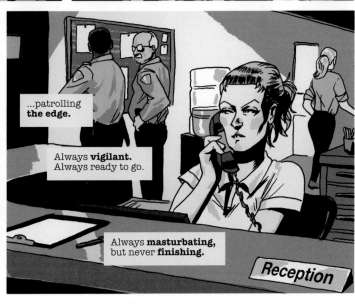

...patrolling **the edge.**

Always **vigilant.** Always ready to go.

Always **masturbating,** but never **finishing.**

Reception

The skell's name is **Todd Stubaker**...

This is his story.

Like all skells, he got bent as a kid and never got **unbent**...

But I guess that's where **we** come in.

Typical family, typical upbringing.

A daddy out there running the rat race, and a mommy...

And so I said—

AAA—

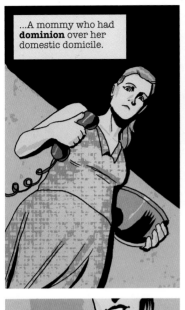

...A mommy who had **dominion** over her domestic domicile.

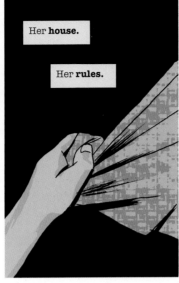

Her **house.**

Her **rules.**

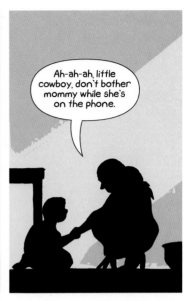

Ah-ah-ah, little cowboy, don't bother mommy while she's on the phone.

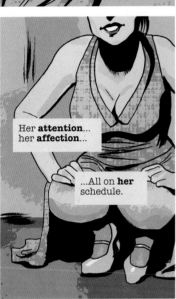

Her **attention**... her **affection**...

...All on **her** schedule.

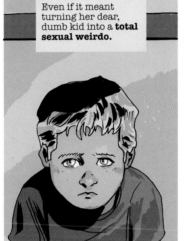

Even if it meant turning her dear, dumb kid into a **total sexual weirdo.**

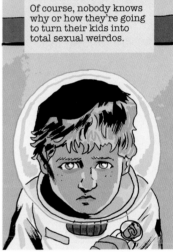

Of course, nobody knows why or how they're going to turn their kids into total sexual weirdos.

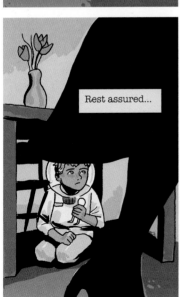

Rest assured...

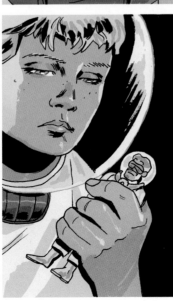

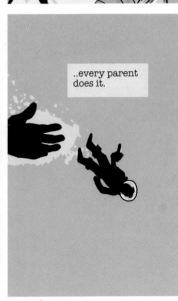

..every parent does it.

Oh GOD DAMN IT!
Sorry honey, Mommy stepped on your toy and broke it.
You've really got to watch where you—
—oh, Christ.
This was the beginning of the little man's fetish.
This was the beginning of **The Little Man.**
To get **mommy's attention...**
...One **brave soldier** after the next would be called upon...
...To make the **ultimate sacrifice.**
I love you too.

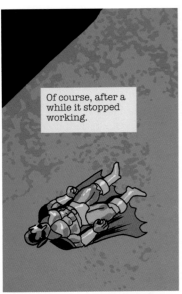

Of course, after a while it stopped working.

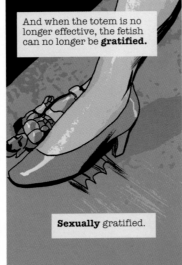

And when the totem is no longer effective, the fetish can no longer be **gratified.**

Sexually gratified.

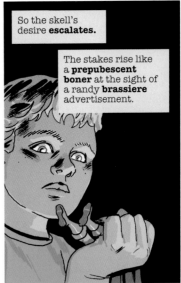

So the skell's desire **escalates.**

The stakes rise like a **prepubescent boner** at the sight of a randy **brassiere** advertisement.

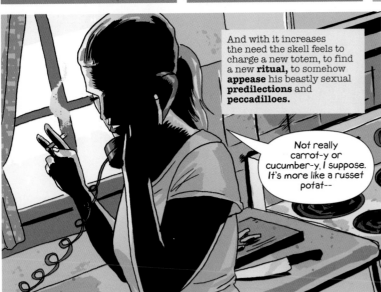

And with it increases the need the skell feels to charge a new totem, to find a new **ritual,** to somehow **appease** his beastly sexual **predilections** and **peccadilloes.**

Not really carrot-y or cucumber-y, I suppose. It's more like a russet potat--

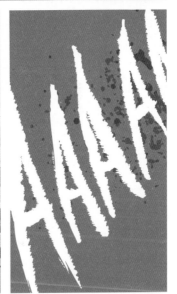

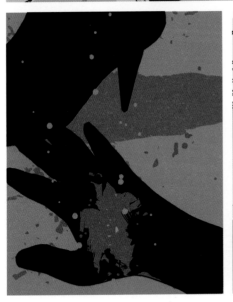

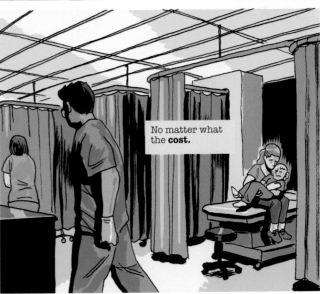

No matter what the **cost.**

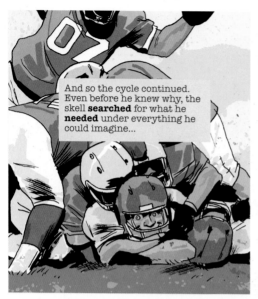

And so the cycle continued. Even before he knew why, the skell **searched** for what he **needed** under everything he could imagine...

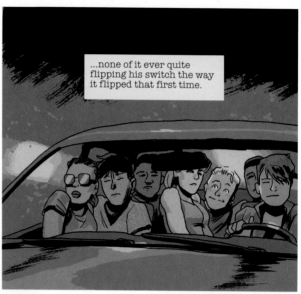

...none of it ever quite flipping his switch the way it flipped that first time.

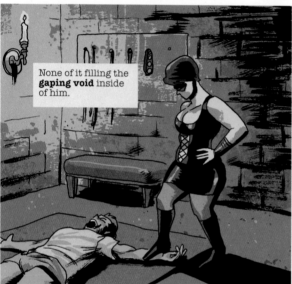

None of it filling the **gaping void** inside of him.

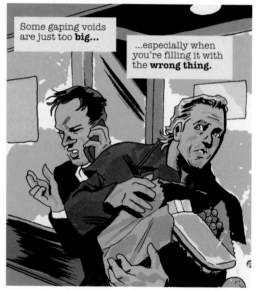

Some gaping voids are just too **big**...

...especially when you're filling it with the **wrong thing**.

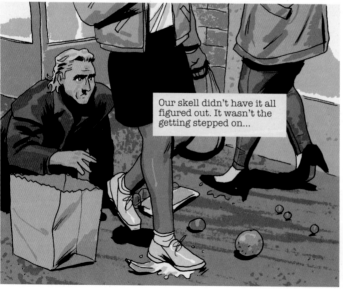

Our skell didn't have it all figured out. It wasn't the getting stepped on...

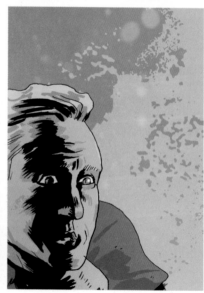

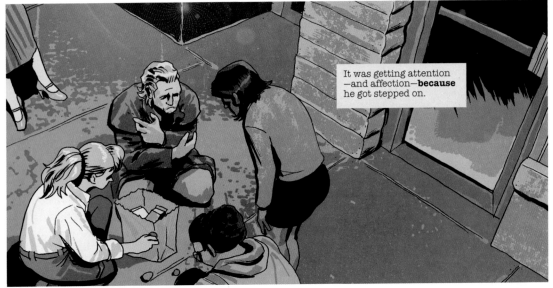

It was getting attention
—and affection—**because**
he got stepped on.

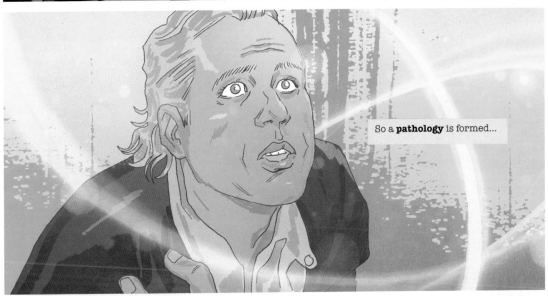

So a **pathology** is formed...

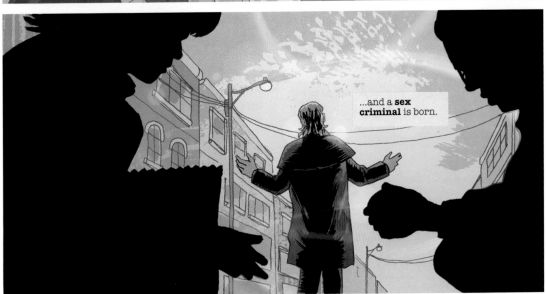

...and a **sex
criminal** is born.

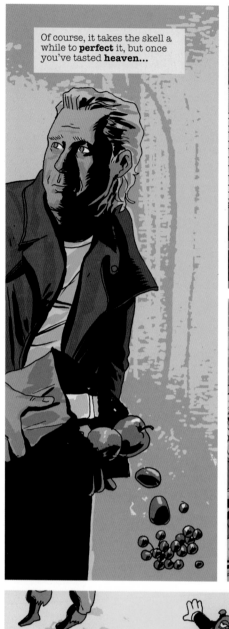

Of course, it takes the skell a while to **perfect** it, but once you've tasted **heaven**...

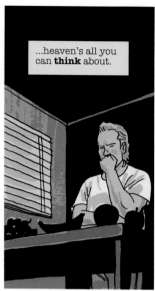

...heaven's all you can **think** about.

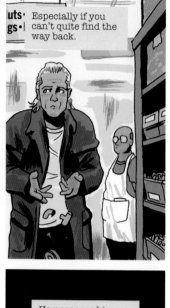

Especially if you can't quite find the way back.

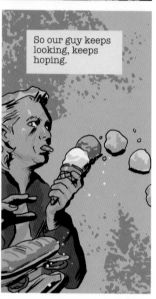

So our guy keeps looking, keeps hoping.

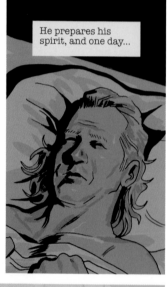

He prepares his spirit, and one day...

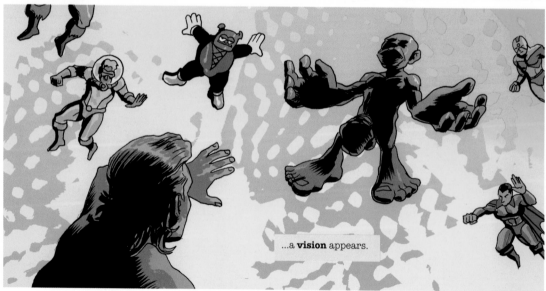

...a **vision** appears.

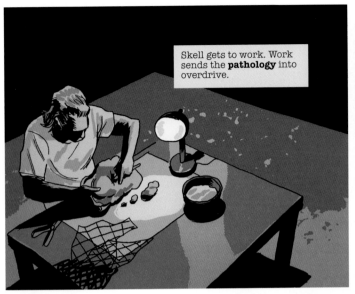

Skell gets to work. Work sends the **pathology** into overdrive.

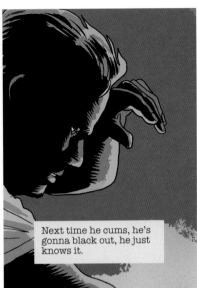

Next time he cums, he's gonna black out, he just knows it.

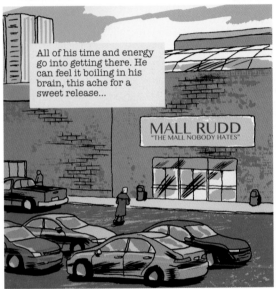

All of his time and energy go into getting there. He can feel it boiling in his brain, this ache for a sweet release...

MALL RUDD
"THE MALL NOBODY HATES"

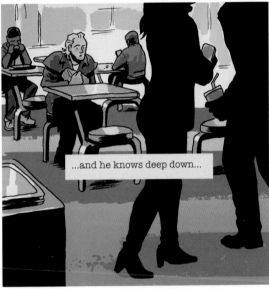

...and he knows deep down...

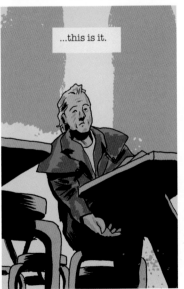

...this is it.

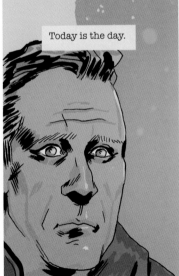

Today is the day.

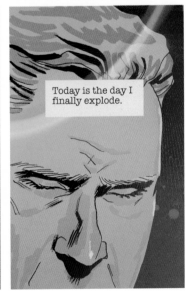

Today is the day I finally explode.

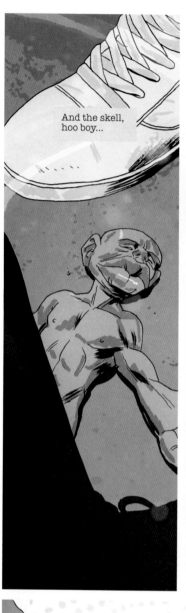

And the skell, hoo boy...

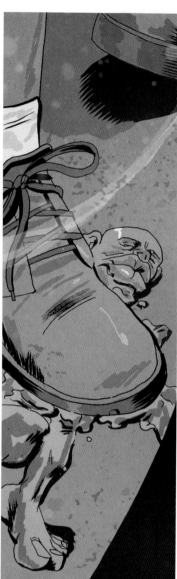

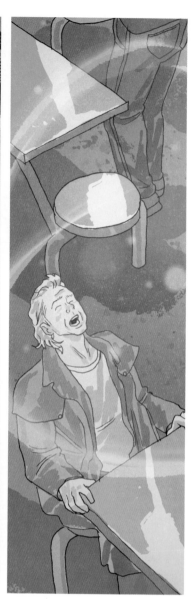

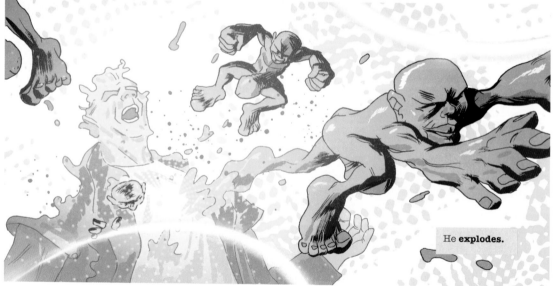

He **explodes.**

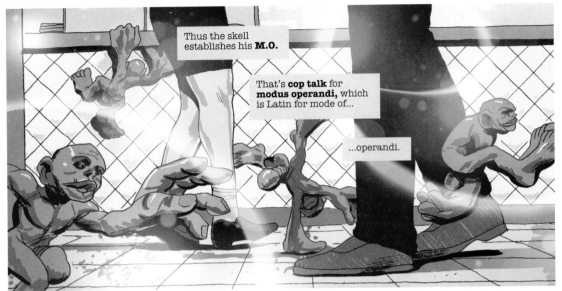

Thus the skell establishes his **M.O.**

That's **cop talk** for **modus operandi,** which is Latin for mode of...

...operandi.

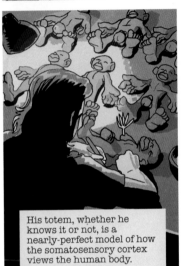

His totem, whether he knows it or not, is a nearly-perfect model of how the somatosensory cortex views the human body.

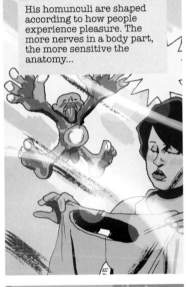

His homunculi are shaped according to how people experience pleasure. The more nerves in a body part, the more sensitive the anatomy...

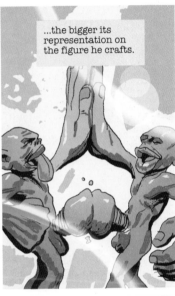

...the bigger its representation on the figure he crafts.

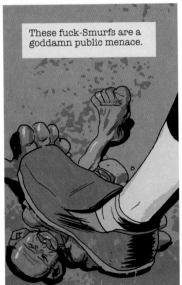

These fuck-Smurfs are a goddamn public menace.

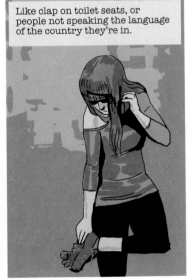

Like clap on toilet seats, or people not speaking the language of the country they're in.

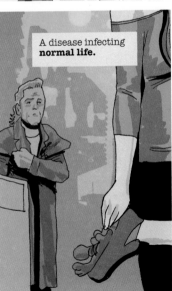

A disease infecting **normal life.**

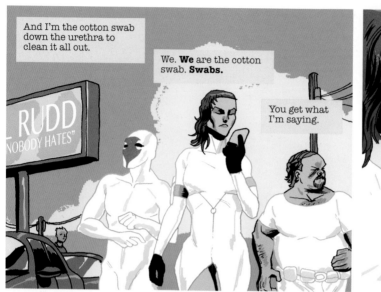

And I'm the cotton swab down the urethra to clean it all out.

We. **We** are the cotton swab. **Swabs.**

You get what I'm saying.

RUDD NOBODY HATES"

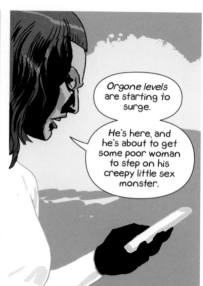

Orgone levels are starting to surge.

He's here, and he's about to get some poor woman to step on his creepy little sex monster.

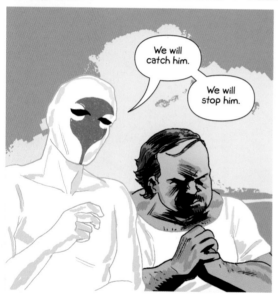

We will catch him.

We will stop him.

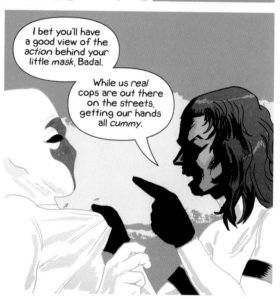

I bet you'll have a good view of the action behind your little mask, Badal.

While us real cops are out there on the streets, getting our hands all cummy.

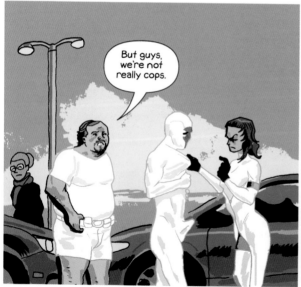

But guys, we're not really cops.

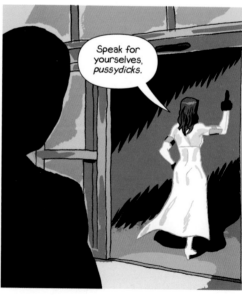

Speak for yourselves, pussydicks.

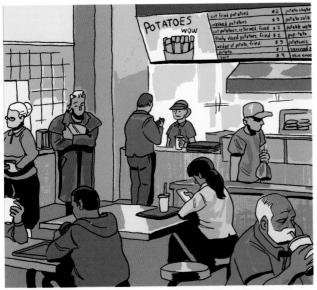

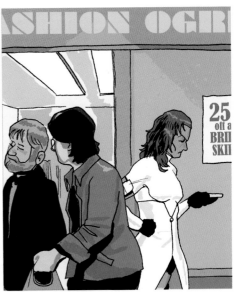

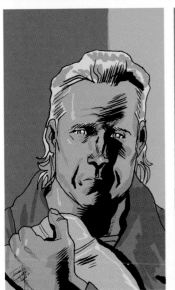

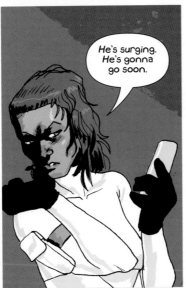

He's surging. He's gonna go soon.

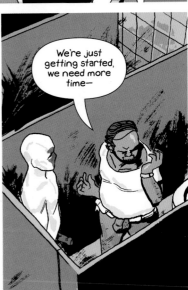

We're just getting started, we need more time—

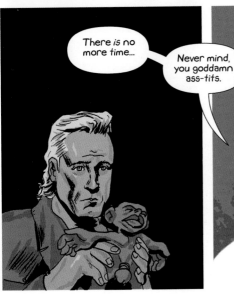

There is no more time...

Never mind, you goddamn ass-tits.

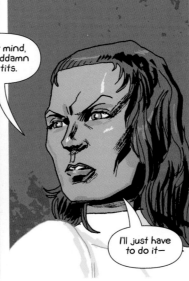

I'll just have to do it—

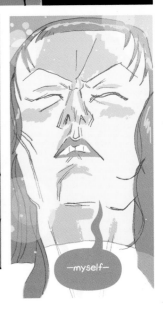

—myself—

My burrito—

FUUUUU

Sex justice stomps down hard with a four-inch heel, creepazoid.

It's like catching **rats** with big **dicks** that want to **fuck** my shoes.

But I **catch** the little Pikachoads.

I catch 'em **all.**

Holy shit!
COOKIE
Shit shit shit shit shit—!!
—shit shit shit shit shit—
You *fool*.
gggurrk
You goddamn fool.
Yeah.
Shut up.
Did you think you were the only one?
You're not.
You get caught, we *all* get caught.
We protect freaks like us from the square world, asshole.
I - I —what—
What do you think happens if people like them learn about people like us?
There—
—there are others?

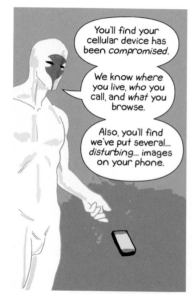
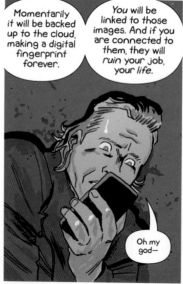
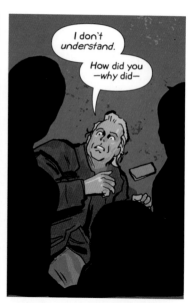

You'll find your cellular device has been *compromised*.

We know *where* you live, *who* you call, and *what* you browse.

Also, you'll find we've put several... *disturbing*... images on your phone.

Momentarily it will be backed up to the cloud, making a digital fingerprint forever.

You will be linked to those images. And if you are connected to them, they will *ruin* your job, your *life*.

Oh my god—

I don't *understand*.

How did you —why did—

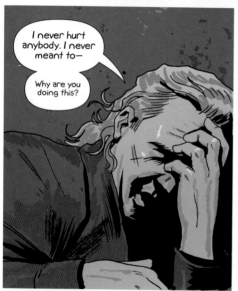
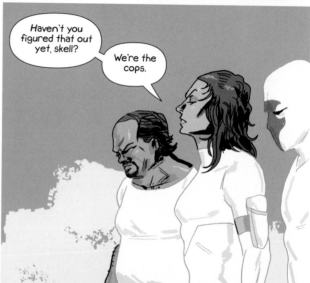

I never hurt anybody. I never meant to—

Why are you doing this?

Haven't you figured that out yet, skell?

We're the cops.

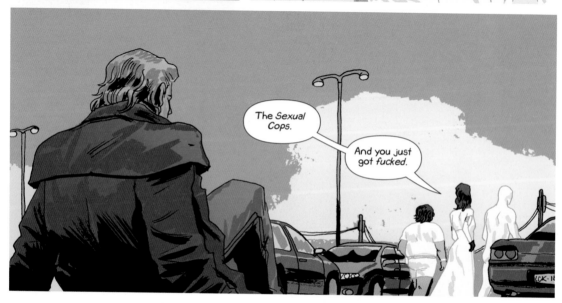

The *Sexual* Cops.

And you just got *fucked*.

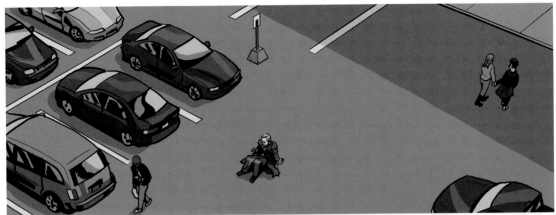

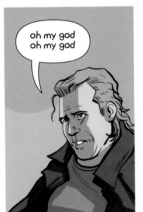

oh my god
oh my god

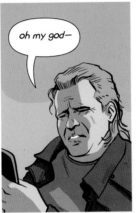

oh my god—

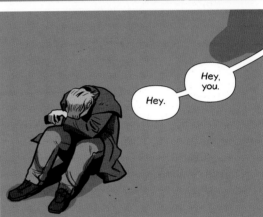

Hey,
you.

Hey.

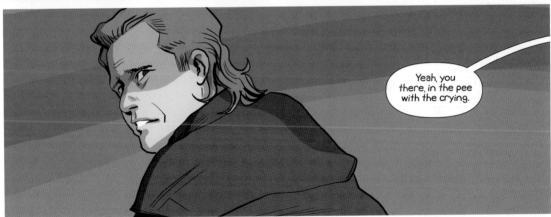

Yeah, you
there, in the pee
with the crying.

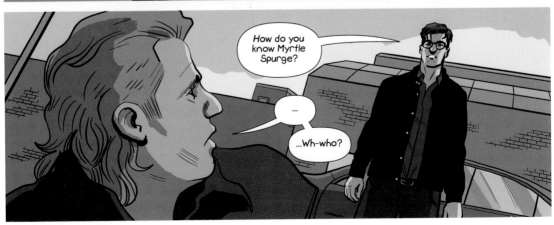

How do you
know Myrtle
Spurge?

...

...Wh-who?

Her. Myrtle Spurge.
Kegelface.
It's cool.
I'm like you.
Who the hell *are* you people?
My name is—
Fuck you!
I know I'm not supposed to care.
I know I'm supposed to be ignoring Kegel and her goons.
I know I'm supposed to be moving on.
I told Suzie I was moving on, that we were moving on...
—but I can't.

MEANWHILE, NEXT CHAPTER:
—AAA GET THEM OFF GET THEM—
What the FUCK—
AMERICA
why you follow me
why
why you follow
why you follow me

18
TOTEMS

MEANWHILE,
LAST CHAPTER:
BRIGHT IDEAS
SINCE 2014
GOODBOY
COOL OLDER BROTHER
SWEETIE STEVE
Oh my.
Oh my.
uh
I got you something.

Was that...
Was that okay?
Yeah, fine. Great.
I mean, we're here, aren't we? Mission accomplished.
No, I mean...
Is there... is there anything you want to do?
That we haven't, I mean.
In bed.
Yes.
No.
You?
Yes.
Nope. No.
No.
There.
We believe that, right?
Yup.
Totally sexually satisfied and comfortable talking about this stuff.
Totally totally comfortable.
Not weird at all.

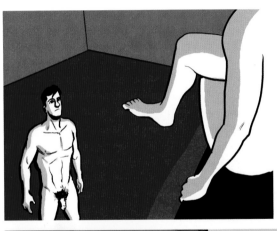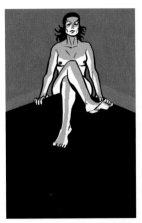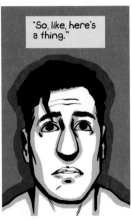

"So, like, here's a thing."

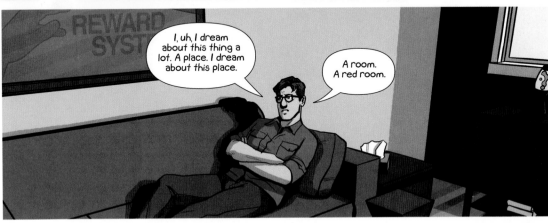

I, uh, I dream about this thing a lot. A place. I dream about this place.

A room. A red room.

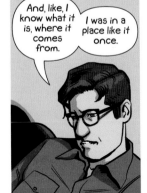

And, like, I know what it is, where it comes from.

I was in a place like it once.

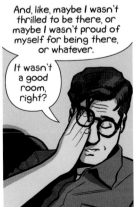

And, like, maybe I wasn't thrilled to be there, or maybe I wasn't proud of myself for being there, or whatever.

It wasn't a good room, right?

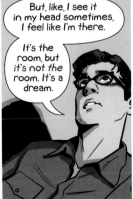

But, like, I see it in my head sometimes, I feel like I'm there.

It's the room, but it's not the room. It's a dream.

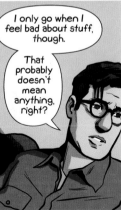

I only go when I feel bad about stuff, though.

That probably doesn't mean anything, right?

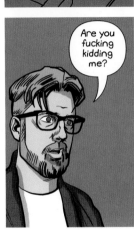

Are you fucking kidding me?

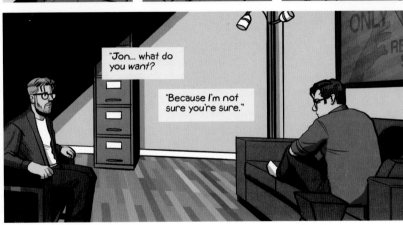

"Jon... what do you want?"

"Because I'm not sure you're sure."

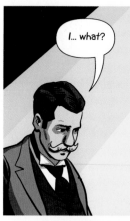

I... what?

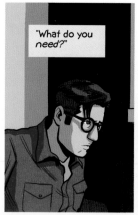

"What do you need?"

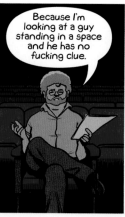

Because I'm looking at a guy standing in a space and he has no fucking clue.

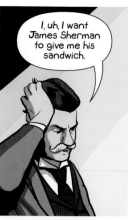

I, uh, I want James Sherman to give me his sandwich.

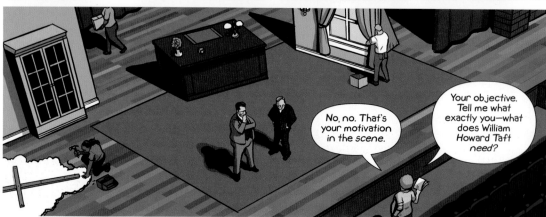

No, no. That's your motivation in the *scene*.

Your objective. Tell me what exactly you—what does William Howard Taft need?

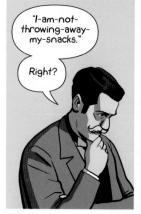

"I-am-not-throwing-away-my-snacks."

Right?

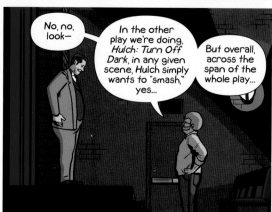

No, no, look—

In the other play we're doing, *Hulch: Turn Off Dark*, in any given scene, Hulch simply wants to "smash," yes...

But overall, across the span of the whole play...

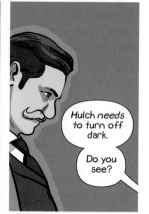

Hulch *needs* to turn off dark.

Do you see?

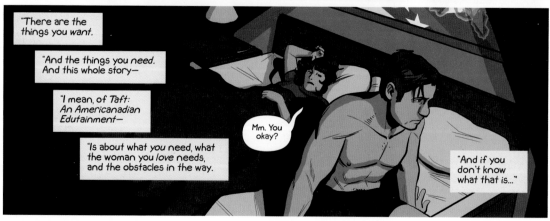

"There are the things you *want*.

"And the things you *need*. And this whole story—

"I mean, of *Taft: An Americanadian Edutainment*—

"Is about what *you* need, what the woman you *love* needs, and the obstacles in the way.

Mm. You okay?

"And if you don't know what that is..."

Just a bad dream.
It's okay.
Go back to sleep.
Anything you want to talk about?
Just.
Just Kegelface.
Ugh, her.
So glad we're done with her.
So glad she's out of our lives.
Yeah.
I'm not thinking about him.

Goddammit, this isn't working.
This isn't working, and I'm not thinking about him.
I'm not thinking about him.
Tautologically iffy, but it's true.
CLASSIFIEDS
I'm not—
God damn it!
—I bet *he* has a car. I bet—
—wonder if *he's* a car guy—
URE FLOR
ALL FLOWERS, ZERO STEMS. GUARANTEED.
DRINK THE WAT
MEXICAN INSPIRED BA
SON OF A BITCH!
—probably not—
THIRTY-FOUR HUNDRED GODDAMN DOLLARS?!?
You know who has money?
BANKCORP BC
SAVINGS NOT MUCH
CHECKING HA HA
LINE OF CREDIT LIKE YOU HAVE THAT
TOTAL BALANCE WHAT ARE YOU, JOKING?
THANK YOU
BANKCORP HAS YOUR MONEY
SUCK A DICK, DUMMY
Doctors have money.
BANKCORP
Don't.
Don't think about him.
APPLETOWN
SEXXXPORGASCON
A CELEBRATION OF FAP CULTURE
SHAKE HANDS WITH THE BEST IN PORN CULTURE—PAST & PRESENT—WITH THE VERY HAND YOU JERK TO THEM WITH!
SATURDAY the 25th, 6-9 ha ha just kidding it's 9-5
$60 GENERAL ADMISSION
$200 "ALL HOLES ACCESS"
note: there is no access to any holes
A CREEPY NEAL INC. PROMOTION
"If it ain't creepy, it ain't Neal"
Don't you fucking do it.

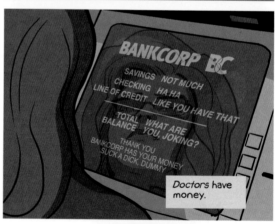

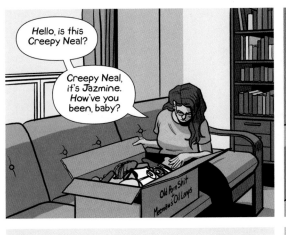

Hello, is this Creepy Neal?

Creepy Neal, it's Jazmine. How've you been, baby?

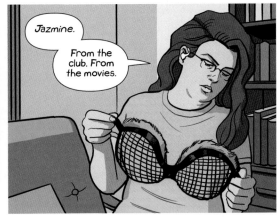

Jazmine.

From the club. From the movies.

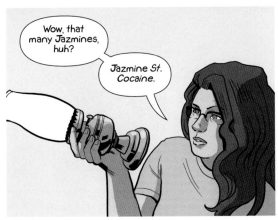

Wow, that many Jazmines, huh?

Jazmine St. Cocaine.

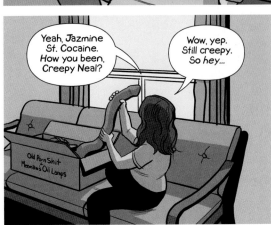

Yeah, Jazmine St. Cocaine. How you been, Creepy Neal?

Wow, yep. Still creepy. So hey...

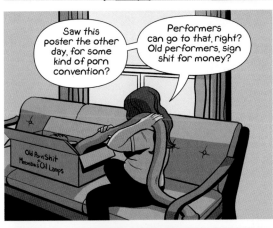

Saw this poster the other day, for some kind of porn convention?

Performers can go to that, right? Old performers, sign shit for money?

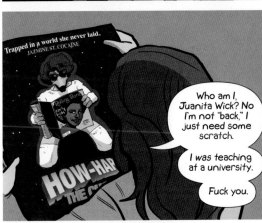

Who am I, Juanita Wick? No I'm not "back," I just need some scratch.

I was teaching at a university.

Fuck you.

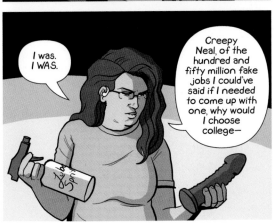

I was. I WAS.

Creepy Neal, of the hundred and fifty million fake jobs I could've said if I needed to come up with one, why would I choose college—

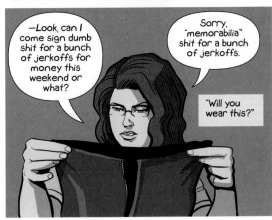

—Look, can I come sign dumb shit for a bunch of jerkoffs for money this weekend or what?

Sorry, "memorabilia" shit for a bunch of jerkoffs.

"Will you wear this?"

I, uh.
I got you something else.
To wear.
Is this okay?
HOT BURGER TEEN
Yeah.
If you're into it, I'm into it.
...Got this for me, didja?
Well.
For us.
Whoa.
Is that okay?
Yeah, just, hoo boy.
For fuck's sake—
WAREHOUSE
DEEP THROAT DISCOUNTS
Can I show you something?
Yeah, but if it's your boobs, I already seen 'em.

Oh, wait, did you vajazzle? Assjazzle?
Are there tiny rhinestones on your b-hole?
Not quite—
AMERICA
But, y'know.
Wow.
Right?
That's quite the collection you have there. This is your thing?
Well.
It's more *Jon's* thing.
That is a *lot* of things.
More like, like it's a lot of kind of the same thing?
Where's the line between "predilection" and "fetish"?
Maybe before your collection hits the four-figures cost point?
Oh shit.
Where's he getting the money for—
Ha ha.
Yeah. *His* job must pay really well.
I mean it's not like he's robbing banks or just stealing the—
Suze.
He couldn't be doing it again.
Could he?
You guys would tell me, right?

Shit.
I'm not his mom. I'm not a cop. But—
—but, goddamn, I have to ask about this, right?
Right?
It's fucked up, all the stuff that can come out of the bottom of an underwear drawer, huh?

Things always feel sad
I wish things would maybe change
But things never ever change
Please please please Oh please
I wish I wish I wish I wish
I wish things didn't feel so sad all the time
Don't think about her.
So sad So sad
I have never felt joy
Ever
What is it
What is joy
Why would I ever feel joy when things are so sad
Don't think—
Don't—
Feminism
—god dammit—
RACH STUFF
Oh it's raining, always raining here, there is always stress
Here in my town which is grey and economically depressed
I don't dream about anything but a small lukewarm cup of tea
With too much milk oh there is always too much milk for me—
—grown-ass man listening to—
—so embarrassing—

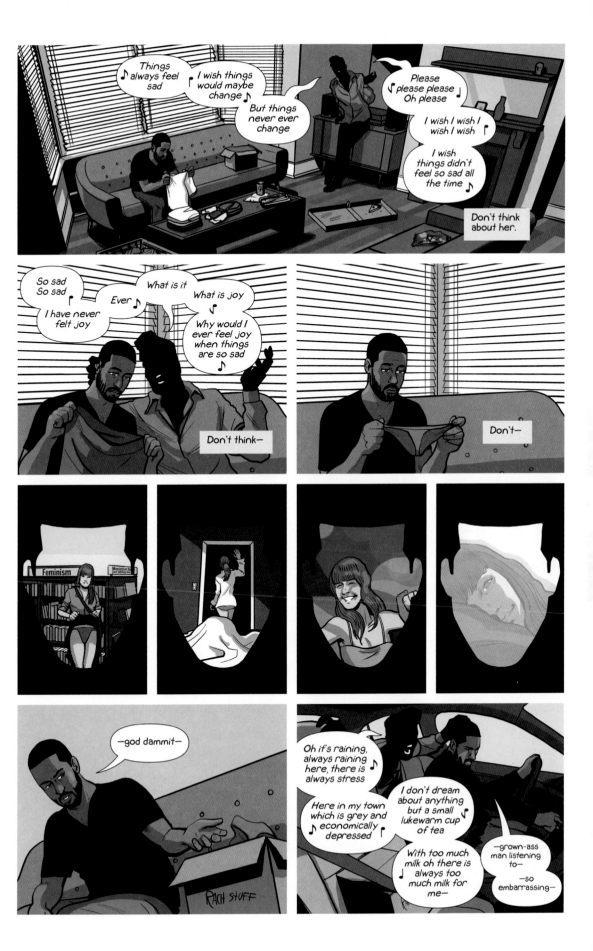

Such an arrassment the scene—
Nng.
YOU CALL ME—
Hey, you.
Hey, uh.
Sorry it took so long for me to get all this stuff together.
Can I come in?

ME:
NDAMENTAL
R EMERGENT?
DR. ANA KINCAID
FRITCHMURRAY
THEATER
4:00P
Join one of Cosmology and Ho
ing stars as she delves into the
Do you spell that with a G or a J, baby?
G.
And, uh...

SEXXXPORGASCON
A CELEBRATION OF FAP CULTURE
THE DREADED NIGHT FUCKER
She ONLY FUCKS at NIGHT
DUKE SCREW
THE KING OF INTERRACIAL DP ON POOL TABLES
(1995-2006)
DUKE SCREW POOL CUE
MASTURBATION IS A SIN!
FUCK ME INSTEAD
JAZMINE ST COCAINE
Don't fucking touch me
LYLE POUNDER
HE FILLED ALL THE HOLES... ...IN YOUR HEART
30
...can I spit on your tits?
BUY HUMPHRIES PENIS WAX
PIX: $20
All you can eat
Olive St. Speed
Her TITS are REAL...
...But her ARM... ...ISN'T!

Are you fucking kidding me?
Oh, sure, I have sex all the time, sex is the best, guys just like you, blah blah.
Sex All The TIME
AAAH goddamn GLITTER in my EYE
Everybody say "BIG TITTIES"!
hey hey HEY
Ugh, what is this, chicken?
I'M EATIN
unclean unclean
JAZMIN
ST. COCAIN
Don't fucking tou
GARY 4 SEX PREZ 2017
Fuck you, Gary.

goddammit
Don't think about him.
Just *stop* for fuck's sake—
Did you really read my paper on interoceptive salience, or do you just want to fuck me because of the porn thing?
...
...Doctor Kincaid?

Yes.
WIFE'S FAVOURITE SONG
DON'T KISS WIFE'S PRETTY FRIEND
Well?
Did you actually read my paper and did it actually change your practice, or am I just that chick from those pornos you used to watch?
I, uh.
I, well. I—
—I, I mean, I know *both* facets of your, uh, of your work—
Sure. You're in my demo, that makes sense.
Look, Doug—
David. Dave.
Why does everybody have such a hard time remembering my name?
Fine, that's on me. Look:
I spent the day in sparkly sausage casing getting breathed on and touched by Jazmine St. Cocaine fans.
I'd really like a drink and maybe dinner with someone who doesn't think about ejaculating on my face whenever I speak.

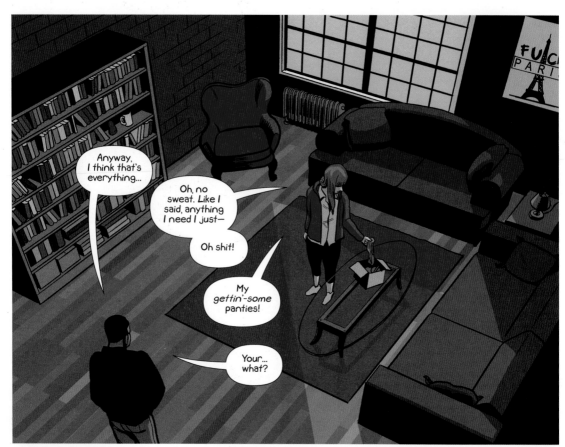

Anyway, I think that's everything...

Oh, no sweat. Like I said, anything I need I just—

Oh shit!

My *gettin'-some* panties!

Your... what?

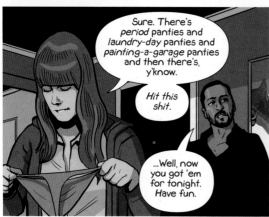

Sure. There's *period* panties and *laundry-day* panties and *painting-a-garage* panties and then there's, y'know.

Hit this shit.

...Well, now you got 'em for tonight. Have fun.

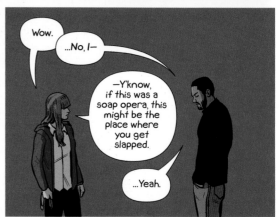

Wow.

...No, I—

—Y'know, if this was a soap opera, this might be the place where you get slapped.

...Yeah.

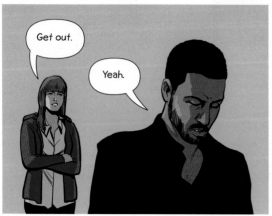

Get out.

Yeah.

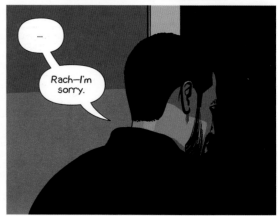

...

Rach—I'm sorry.

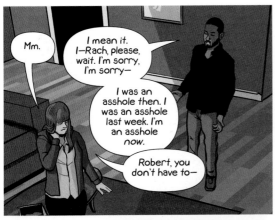

Mm.

I mean it. I—Rach, please, wait. I'm sorry, I'm sorry—

I was an asshole then. I was an asshole last week. I'm an asshole now.

Robert, you don't have to—

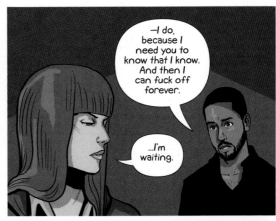

—I do, because I need you to know that I know. And then I can fuck off forever.

...I'm waiting.

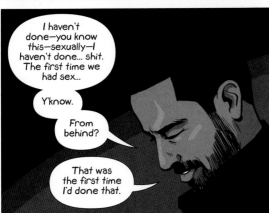

I haven't done—you know this—sexually—I haven't done... shit. The first time we had sex...

Y'know.

From behind?

That was the first time I'd done that.

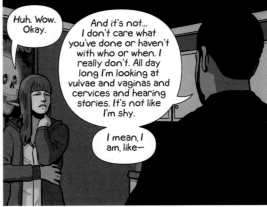

Huh. Wow. Okay.

And it's not... I don't care what you've done or haven't with who or when. I really don't. All day long I'm looking at vulvae and vaginas and cervices and hearing stories. It's not like I'm shy.

I mean, I am, like—

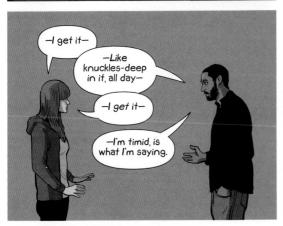

—I get it—

—Like knuckles-deep in it, all day—

—I get it—

—I'm timid, is what I'm saying.

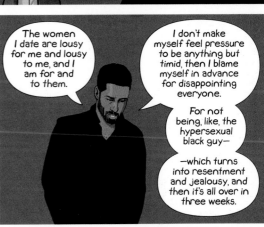

The women I date are lousy for me and lousy to me, and I am for and to them.

I don't make myself feel pressure to be anything but timid, then I blame myself in advance for disappointing everyone.

For not being, like, the hypersexual black guy—

—which turns into resentment and jealousy, and then it's all over in three weeks.

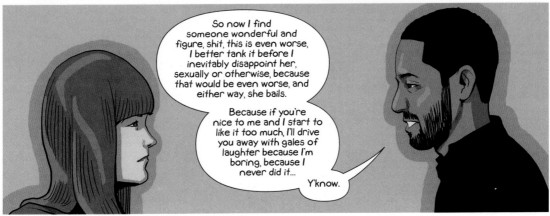

So now I find someone wonderful and figure, shit, this is even worse, I better tank it before I inevitably disappoint her, sexually or otherwise, because that would be even worse, and either way, she bails.

Because if you're nice to me and I start to like it too much, I'll drive you away with gales of laughter because I'm boring, because I never did it...

Y'know.

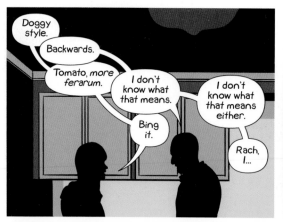

Doggy style.

Backwards.

Tomato, *more ferarum.*

I don't know what that means.

Bing it.

I don't know what that means either.

Rach, I...

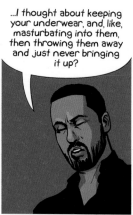

...I thought about keeping your underwear, and, like, masturbating into them, then throwing them away and just never bringing it up?

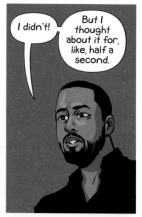

I didn't!

But I thought about it for, like, half a second.

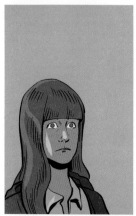

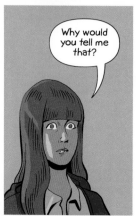

Why would you tell me that?

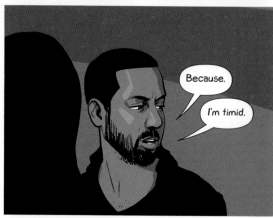

Because.

I'm timid.

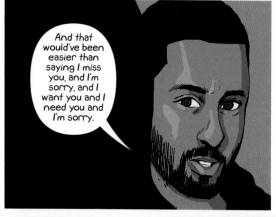

And that would've been easier than saying I miss you, and I'm sorry, and I want you and I need you and I'm sorry.

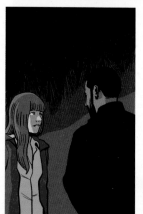

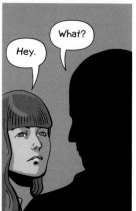

Hey.

What?

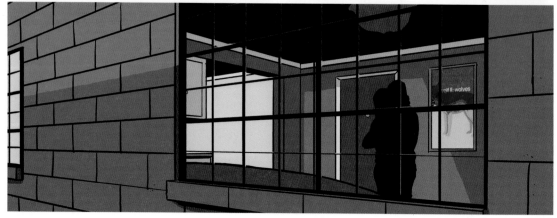

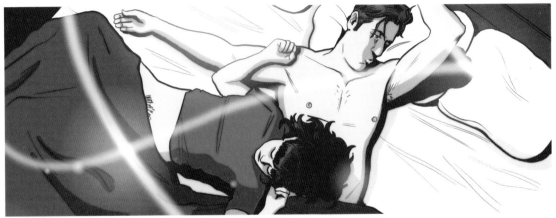

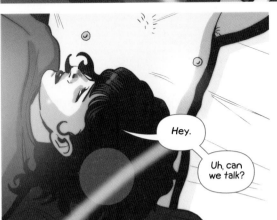

Hey.

Uh, can we talk?

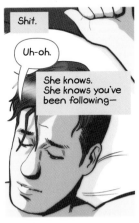

Shit.

Uh-oh.

She knows. She knows you've been following—

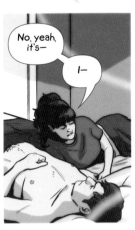

No, yeah, it's—

I—

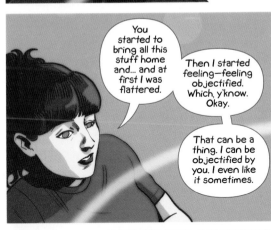

You started to bring all this stuff home and... and at first I was flattered.

Then I started feeling—feeling objectified. Which, y'know. Okay.

That can be a thing. I can be objectified by you. I even like it sometimes.

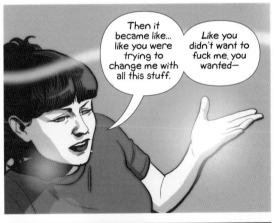

Then it became like... like you were trying to change me with all this stuff.

Like you didn't want to fuck me, you wanted—

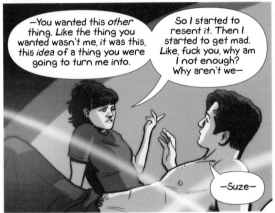

—You wanted this other thing. Like the thing you wanted wasn't me, it was this, this idea of a thing you were going to turn me into.

So I started to resent it. Then I started to get mad. Like, fuck you, why am I not enough? Why aren't we—

—Suze—

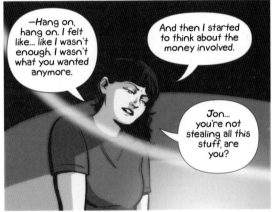

—Hang on, hang on. I felt like... like I wasn't enough. I wasn't what you wanted anymore.

And then I started to think about the money involved.

Jon... you're not stealing all this stuff, are you?

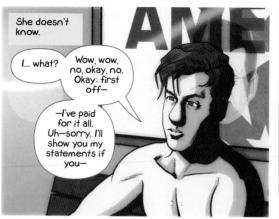

She doesn't know.

I... what?

Wow, wow, no, okay, no. Okay: first off—

—I've paid for it all. Uh—sorry. I'll show you my statements if you—

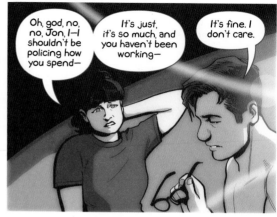

Oh, god, no, no, Jon, I—I shouldn't be policing how you spend—

It's just, it's so much, and you haven't been working—

It's fine. I don't care.

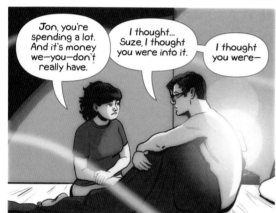

Jon, you're spending a lot. And it's money we—you—don't really have.

I thought... Suze, I thought you were into it.

I thought you were—

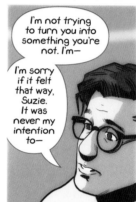

I'm not trying to turn you into something you're not. I'm—

I'm sorry if it felt that way, Suzie. It was never my intention to—

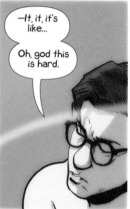

—It, it, it's like...

Oh, god this is hard.

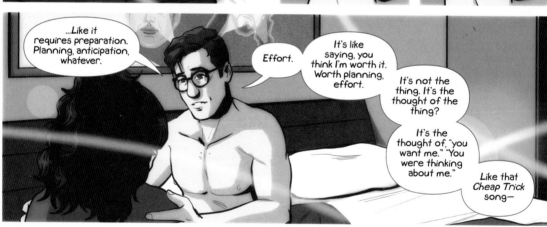

...Like it requires preparation. Planning, anticipation, whatever.

Effort.

It's like saying, you think I'm worth it. Worth planning, effort.

It's not the thing. It's the thought of the thing?

It's the thought of, "you want me." "You were thinking about me."

Like that *Cheap Trick* song—

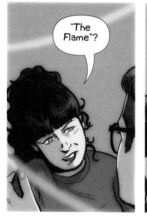

"The Flame"?

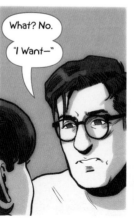

What? No.

"I Want—"

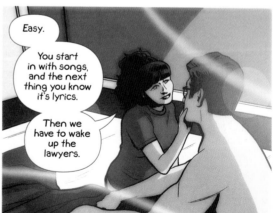

Easy.

You start in with songs, and the next thing you know it's lyrics.

Then we have to wake up the lawyers.

Mm.
Yes. Like that Cheap Trick song, "The Flame."
"I want you to want... 'the flame.'"
"I need you to need... 'the... flame.'"
Did you know Audi used slave labor from German concentration camps to build their cars during the war?
The same Audi that used Queen's anthemic *"We Are the Champions"* in a commercial?
The *very* same! Thank god Freddie didn't live to see that most un-Queen-worthy use of their song.
You're all I want. And I like being wanted, is all.
Just promise you're done with all that other shit? The stealing, the bank, Kegelface—
What do you *want?*
Uh-huh!
Whew.
Okay.
I feel wanted. I just... I just don't want to feel... augmented. Can we take a break from all that?
Yeah, of course.
You piece of shit.
G'night.
G'night, baby.
Lying sack of SHIT—

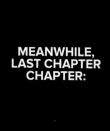

MEANWHILE,
LAST CHAPTER
CHAPTER:

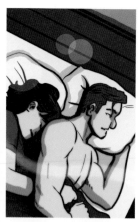
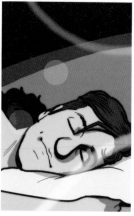
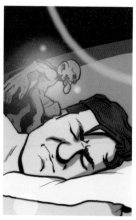
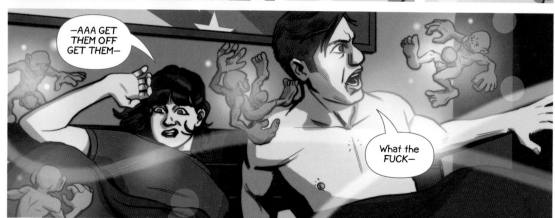
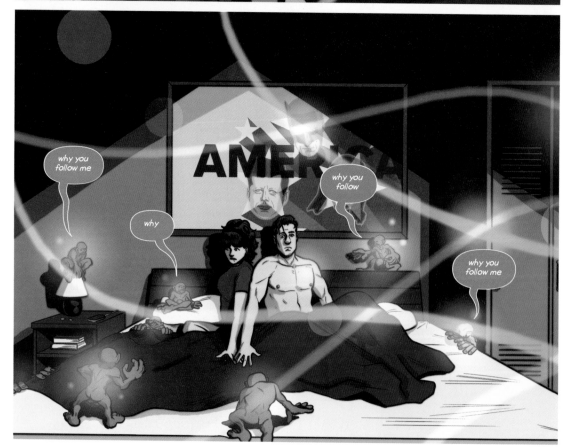

DOWN
WITH THE
THICKNESS

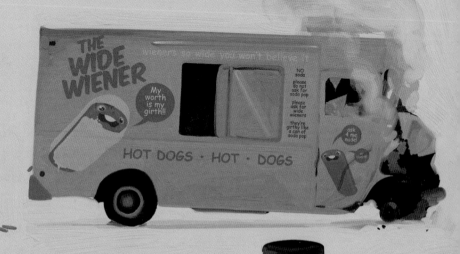

WIENER
URRY!
WIDE!
FUCKING!
WIENER!
MAAAAAAN!
I might be short, but I'm so wide So wide that I won't fit in-side
Take your time and gen-tl-y Soon inside your mouth I'll be!
Wide Wieners! Wide Wieners! Stubby, jolly, full of mirth!
Wide Wieners! Wide Wieners! I'm not long but I have girth!
TERTIARY SECONDARY
THE WIDE WIENER
HOT DOGS · HOT · DOGS
Wieners aren't one size fits all Long fat short bent big or small
Just be cool and trust me chum! I'm a wiener made for buns!
My worth is my girth!!
wide you won't believe it
HOT DOGS
HOT DOGS
NO soda
please do not ask for soda pop
please ask for wide wieners
they're girthy like a can of soda pop
ask 4 me nude!
So wide that I won't fit in-side
your mouth I'll be!
of mirth!
I'm not long but I have girth!
My worth is my girth!!
oh no
please do not ask for soda pop
please ask for wide wieners
they're girthy like a can of soda pop

but I'm so wide
So wide that I
won't fit inside
your mouth I'll be!
oh no—
sllllurp
My worth is my girth!!
slammo!
—no no no no—
Hey, mister—
please do not ask for soda po
please ask for wide wieners
they're girthy lik a can of soda po
Mister, wait!
We want wide wieners!
I NEED YOUR WIDE WIENER RIGHT NOWWW!
GOD IS DEAD AND HE—
HATES.
USSS

So...
...so are we just not gonna talk?
Like...
...at all?
What is there to talk about?
You lied to me.
I didn't *lie*-lie to you.
I just... didn't tell you.
A lie by omission is still a lie, goddammit.
There's a reason you didn't tell me.
Here, we're *here*—
...whaaaaat the fuck, Jon.

SEXY STUFF
NO SEXY STUFF
CFS COVERED FULL SERVICE INSURANCE CO. CFS
AMUSEMEN
TICKETS
We were supposed to be *done* with weird shit, Jon.
I'm not too sure the weird shit is done with us, babe.
JACK-A-MOLE
"Babe."
Feh.
Don't.
—There he is.

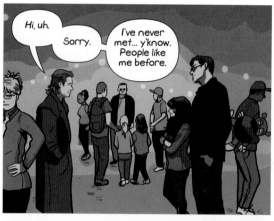

Hi, uh.

Sorry.

I've never met... y'know. People like me before.

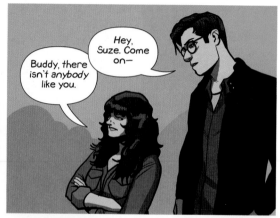

Buddy, there isn't *anybody* like you.

Hey, Suze. Come on—

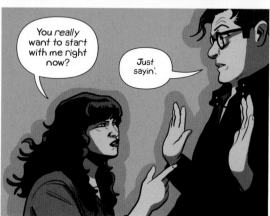

You *really* want to start with me right now?

Just sayin'.

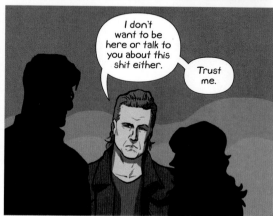

I don't want to be here or talk to you about this shit either.

Trust me.

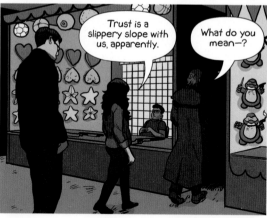

Trust is a slippery slope with us, apparently.

What do you mean—?

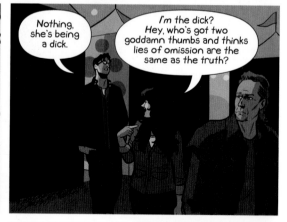

Nothing, she's being a dick.

I'm the dick? Hey, who's got two goddamn thumbs and thinks lies of omission are the same as the truth?

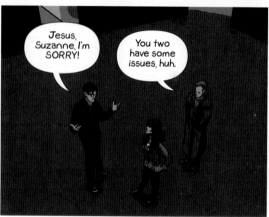

Jesus, Suzanne, I'm SORRY!

You two have some issues, huh.

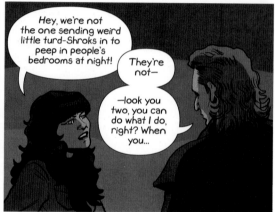

Hey, we're not the one sending weird little turd-Shroks in to peep in people's bedrooms at night!

They're not—

—look you two, you can do what I do, right? When you...

Turd. Shroks.
They're somatosensory maps of—
You know what? Don't have to explain myself to you.
Just tell me how to get away from...
Her.
We call her 'Kegelface' because...
Well, kegel face.
She can hunt down and sniff out people like us—
Jesus.
I thought it was just me.
Then us.
There's more?
Jesus.
Look, man, I'm sorry. I never wanted—I'm sorry. It's the only way...
...I know it's gross but it's the only way I can.
Just tell your boss to leave me alone, I'll—
"Boss"? "Tell"? The fuck?
Buddy, we don't work for her, she—
Oh, fuck you guys.
You set me up!
—The hell?

...
Eat shit, titdicks!
Hey—the Shrokfucker took off.

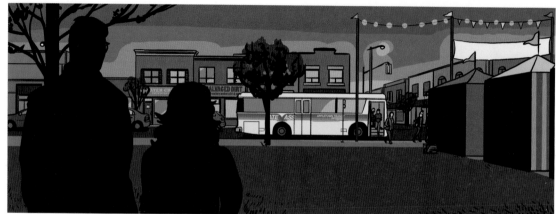

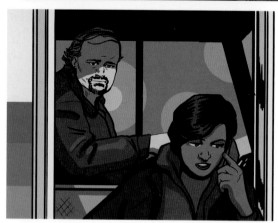

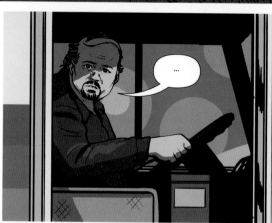

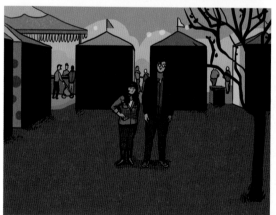

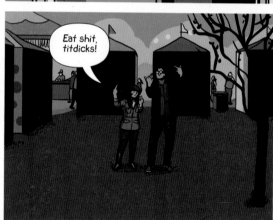

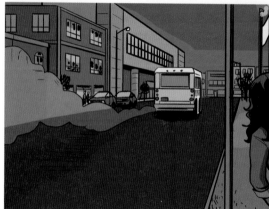

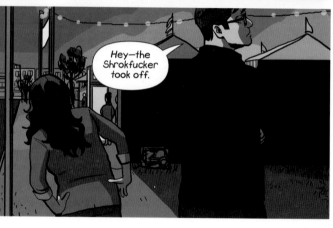

BADALCORP
Beta testing these data streams required some peer management in the knowledge density department, but as I think you'll see—
—there's a real value proposition here in incentivizing our user's privacy-ecologies.
You may be asking yourselves—
"But, Kuber Badal, you're a fabulously wealthy thoughtovation innoventor! Why do you need us?"
In a word?
Horizontally-integrated disruptive value-optics.
COLLATION
Infocologies are the new landscape. We are seeking globally-evolved, hyperscaled quality-vectors outside of our own paradigm.
Simple, really.
Synthigrating the dynamic knowledge-feeds of BankCorp's leveraged target communities with BadalCorp's handheld-slash-mobile data curation and unprivacy nodes gives us incomplete concept-variables.
This is where *you* come in.
I don't need money. I need partners.
Take this average, randomly selected client we selected totally at random and for no other reason.

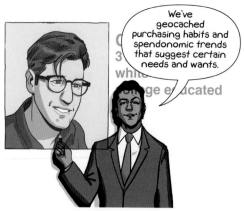
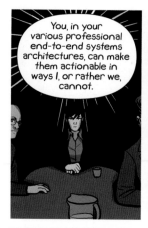
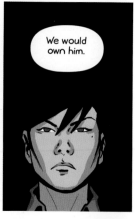

We've geocached purchasing habits and spendonomic trends that suggest certain needs and wants.

You, in your various professional end-to-end systems architectures, can make them actionable in ways I, or rather we, cannot.

We would own him.

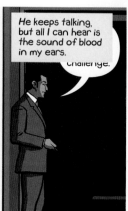
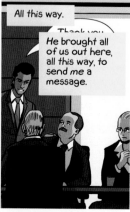
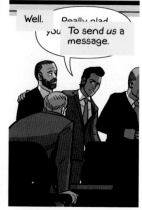
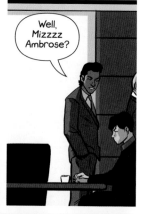

He keeps talking, but all I can hear is the sound of blood in my ears.

All this way.

He brought all of us out here, all this way, to send me a message.

Well.

Really glad you To send us a message.

Well, Mizzzz Ambrose?

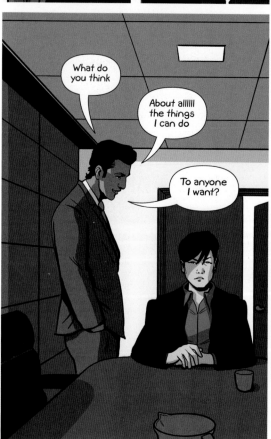
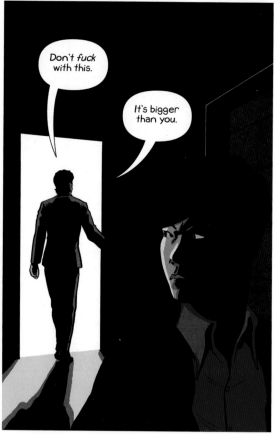

What do you think

About alllll the things I can do

To anyone I want?

Don't fuck with this.

It's bigger than you.

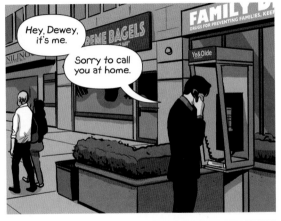

Hey, Dewey, it's me.

Sorry to call you at home.

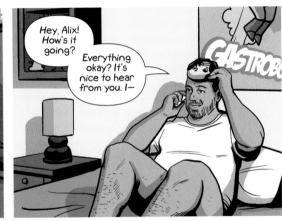

Hey, Alix! How's it going?

Everything okay? It's nice to hear from you. I—

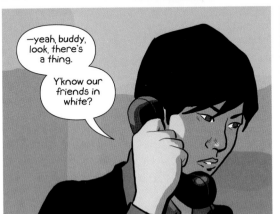

—yeah, buddy, look, there's a thing.

Y'know our friends in white?

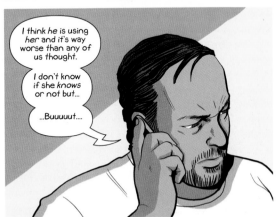

I think *he* is using *her* and it's way worse than any of us thought.

I don't know if she *knows* or not but...

...Buuuuut....

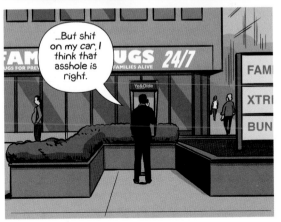

...But shit on my *car*, I think that asshole is right.

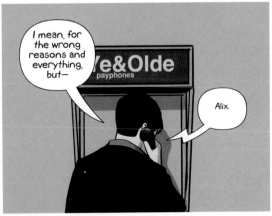

I mean, for the wrong reasons and everything, but—

Alix.

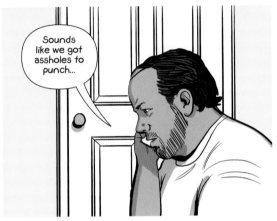

Sounds like we got assholes to punch...

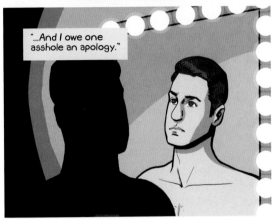

"...And I owe one asshole an apology."

Wait, what the hell is going on here again?
I don't think this idea is gonna work.
Well, it has to, Jon! Okay?! It has to.
Legal concerns and budget cuts mean both of our plays this season have been combined.
Taft: An Americanadian Edutainment and Hulch: Turn Off Dark are therefore now known as HUFTCH: TURN OFF CANADA! And that's fucking that.
So are you with me or against me, shitnoodles?
WAR
LL-NIGHT PANTS
Yeah, man, something's missing.
This is never gonna work.
Sorry.

Something's missing, something's missing.
What missing, chum? Me as solicitor general of United States?
What? No, not you, Incrandleberry Huftch.
what's missing jon what's missing...
Me know!
Rousing hip-hop show tune where Supreme Court justice get punched with car—
No! Get out of my head! Nobody cares about you.
I got this whole other thing I'm talking about.
This is missing.
You *like* it in here, and you know it.
...Shit.
Shit.
Shit.
Yes! HUFTCH AM NOT THROWING AWAY HIM—FIAT!

Oh.
Hey.
Hey.
Uh...
A short-sleeved casual top, generally made of cotton, having the shape of a T when spread out flat.
I, uh...
How was your day?
Fine.
I gotta go out.
Annnnnd shit.

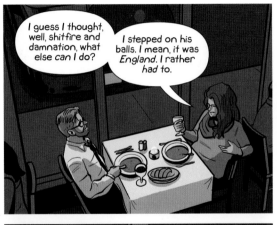

I guess I thought, well, shitfire and damnation, what else *can* I do?

I stepped on his balls. I mean, it was *England*. I rather had to.

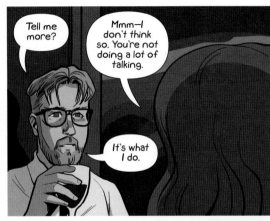

Tell me more?

Mmm—I don't think so. You're not doing a lot of talking.

It's what I do.

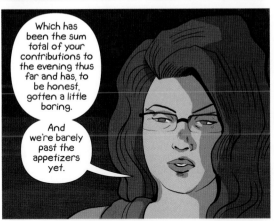

It's what you do with patients.

Don't treat me like a patient.

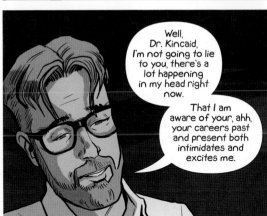

Of course not. I just—it's habit.

Well, break it. Tell me something.

What would you like to hear?

At this point, literally anything other than "Mm-hm" or "Why do you think that is?"

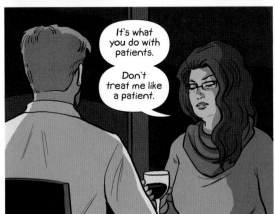

Which has been the sum total of your contributions to the evening thus far and has, to be honest, gotten a little boring.

And we're barely past the appetizers yet.

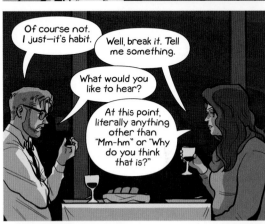

Well, Dr. Kincaid, I'm not going to lie to you, there's a lot happening in my head right now.

That I am aware of your, ahh, your careers past and present both intimidates and excites me.

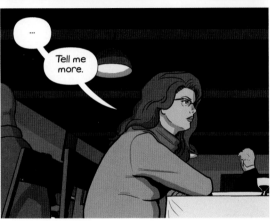

...

Tell me more.

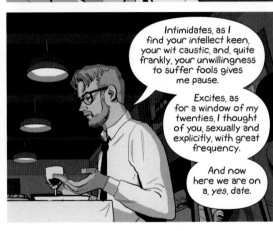

Intimidates, as I find your intellect keen, your wit caustic, and, quite frankly, your unwillingness to suffer fools gives me pause.

Excites, as for a window of my twenties, I thought of you, sexually and explicitly, with great frequency.

And now here we are on a, *yes*, date.

A first date at that, but that context and its spectra of suggestions, combined with my personal history with the idea of you, has cast an inescapable sexual pall over the evening that goes beyond the stereotypical, "will I get laid tonight?" and into a place of having a meal across a table from one's sexual fantasy.
Albeit twenty-some years on.
This is a combination of cowardice and fear of rejection for reasons of inadequacies, sexual, intellectual, or otherwise, I know, but knowing doesn't lessen their impact.
Lastly, I think it's fair to say, and an open secret, that I'm a little bit rebound-y at just this moment. While my previous relationship was not a great font of emotional well-being and health, we were, sexually, extraordinarily compatible and I did, despite myself, like her and I am aware that you, for reasons I do not understand, do not.
So to loop back around, then, it's impossible to not at least, even a little, hypothetically compare and contrast a real woman, with whom I had at least some kind of relationship, with not you but my idea of you, as a figure of fantasy and wish fulfillment— both sexually and intellectually.
And I am acutely aware of how unfair that is, if not downright insulting and belittling, as none of it has anything to do with you—the actual you, the real you—and everything to do with me, being a self-obsessed dick.
Which I believe is the textbook definition of a shitty first date.
All of which is a long way of saying, I'm waiting for the butterflies in my stomach to go away and my mouth to stop being so goddamn dry.

That was good.

GUY
The hell?
"DEAR GUY SORRY I DON'T KNOW YOUR NAME I AM SORRY I FOLLOWED YOU I AM SORRY FOR EVERYTHING I PROMISE IF I SURVIVE I WILL NEVER DO IT AGAIN BUT FOR NOW I AM SO ASHAMED AND AFRAID I AM DOING THE ONLY THING I CAN I'M SORRY I'M SORRY I NEVER MEANT TO HURT ANYONE I'M SORRY
"PLEASE DON'T TELL MY MOTHER I HOPE THIS JUST LOOKS LIKE AN ACCIDENT I DON'T WANT TO UPSET HER"
Shit.
Running is Actually Quite Good For You
269
SHIT!

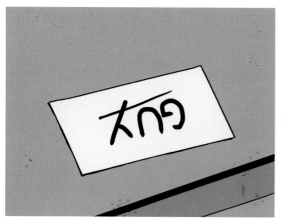

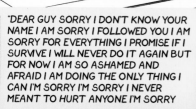

I might be short, but I'm so wide So wide that I won't fit in-side
THE WIDE WIENER
Take your time and gen-tl-y Soon inside your mouth I'll be!
Wide Wieners! Wide Wieners! Stubby, jolly, full of mirth!
Wide Wieners! Wide Wieners! I'm not long but I have girth!
Wieners aren't one size fits all Long fat short bent big or small
Just be cool and trust me chum!
I'm a wiener made for buns

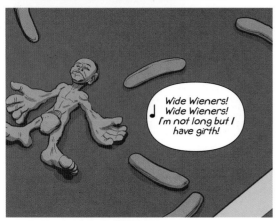

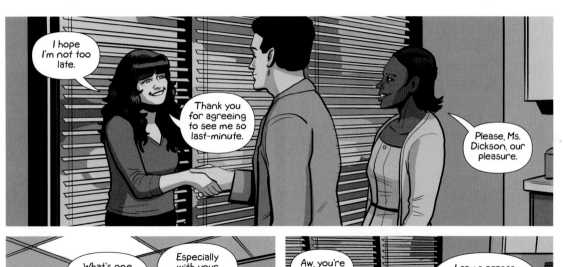

I hope I'm not too late.

Thank you for agreeing to see me so last-minute.

Please, Ms. Dickson, our pleasure.

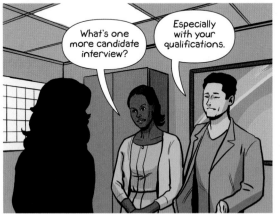

What's one more candidate interview?

Especially with your qualifications.

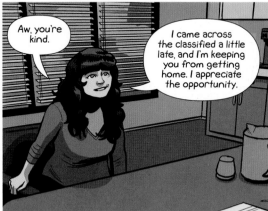

Aw, you're kind.

I came across the classified a little late, and I'm keeping you from getting home. I appreciate the opportunity.

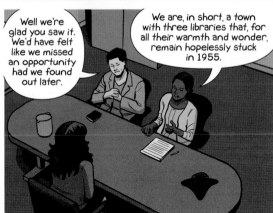

Well we're glad you saw it. We'd have felt like we missed an opportunity had we found out later.

We are, in short, a town with three libraries that, for all their warmth and wonder, remain hopelessly stuck in 1955.

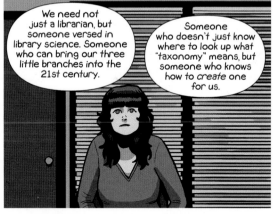

We need not just a librarian, but someone versed in library science. Someone who can bring our three little branches into the 21st century.

Someone who doesn't just know where to look up what "taxonomy" means, but someone who knows how to create one for us.

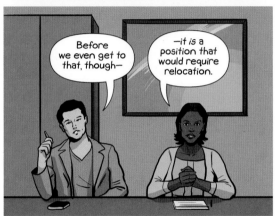

Before we even get to that, though—

—it is a position that would require relocation.

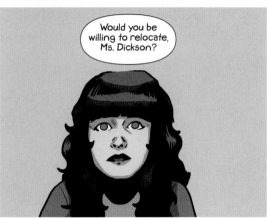

Would you be willing to relocate, Ms. Dickson?

Yes.
Yes I would.

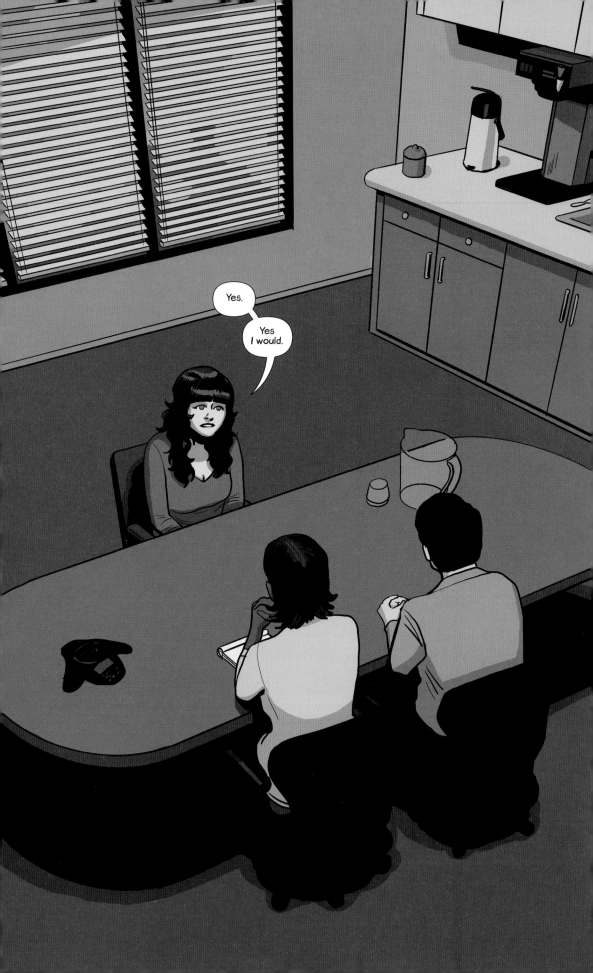

Well, shit.

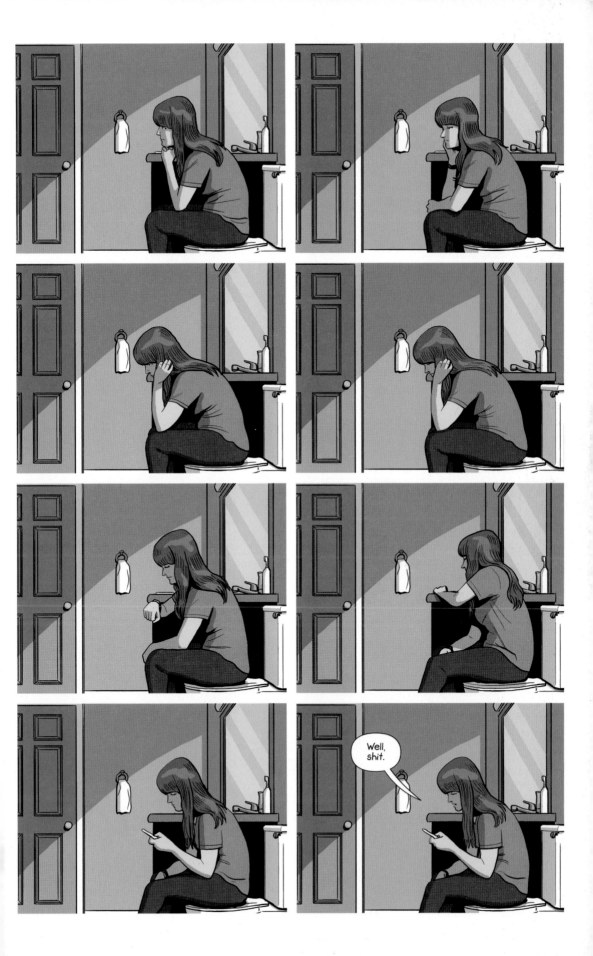

20
OUTS

Fuck.
I don't want to do this.
THE WIDE
POLICE

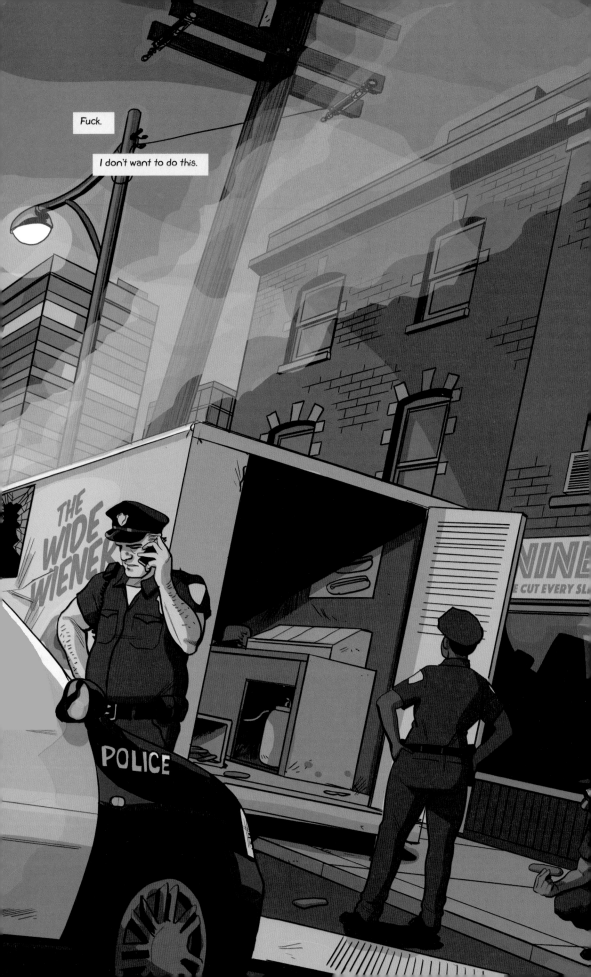

ONE PIZZA
NINE SMALLER SLICES, GUARANTEED
Running is Actually Quite Good For You

It's been coming for a while now.
I really don't want to do this.

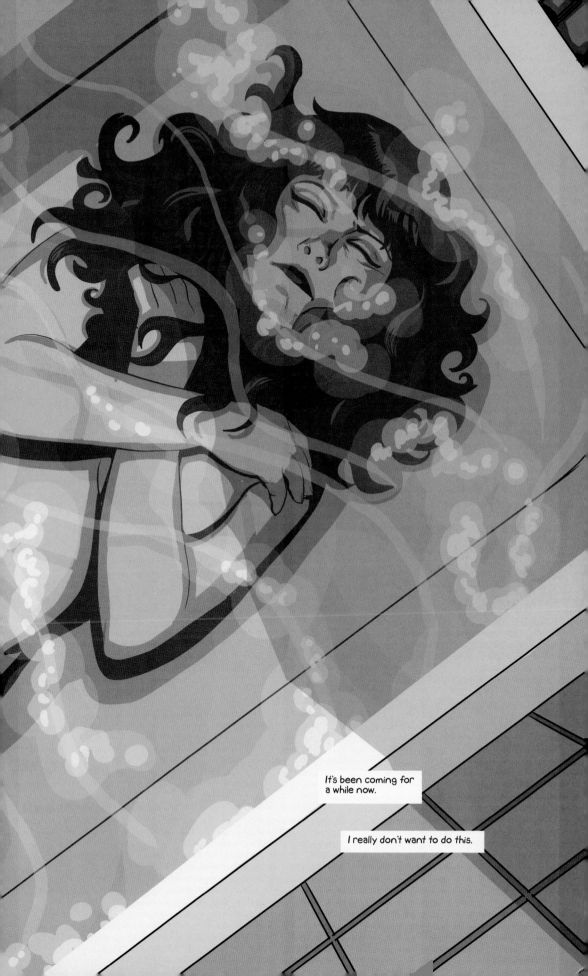

TODD PWNED MEMEORIAL
SORRY
Running is Actually Quite Good For You
cornichon

THE CHRISTIAN WARD
ALL FAITHS WELCOME
jk just christians
Running is Actually Quite Good For You
SORRY

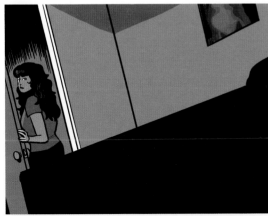

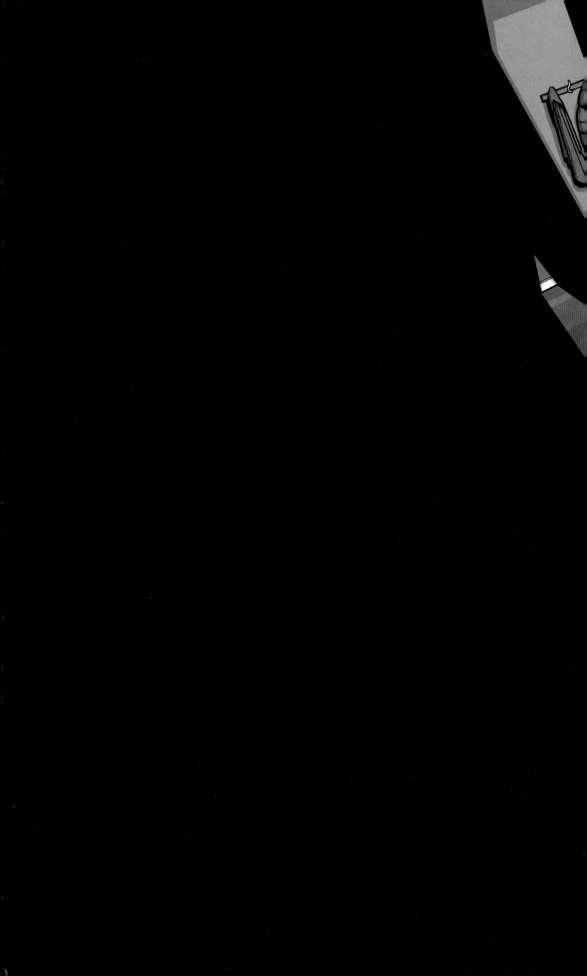

Hey.
Hey.
So, uh.
We should talk.
Yeah.
Let's talk.

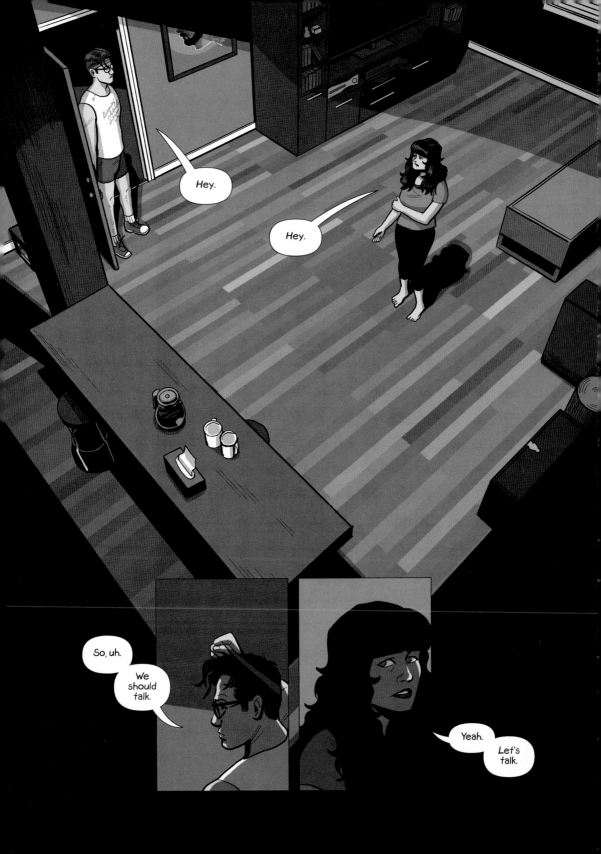

HEART BREAKER
Nnnf.
I gotta stop.
My jaw is gonna fall off.
Yeah.
Besides, your beard exfoliated my pussy to shreds and you sound like a horse eating a sugar cube.
Ooph, I'm tired.
I'm sorry. I really wanted to make you cum.
No you didn't.
You *needed* to make me cum.
Uh...
Excuse me?
You were competing with all these things in your head you think sex with "me" means. But that's sex with an *idea*, not a person.
That's not about *want*. That's about *need*.
That wasn't sex about *me* and it sure as shit wasn't sex about *us*.
It was sex about *you* and your *need*.

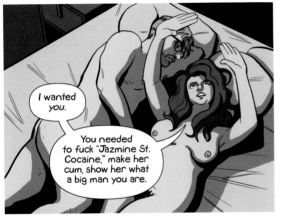

I wanted *you*.

You needed to fuck "Jazmine St. Cocaine," make her cum, show her what a big man you are.

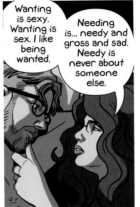

Wanting is sexy. Wanting is sex. I like being wanted.

Needing is... needy and gross and sad. Needy is never about someone else.

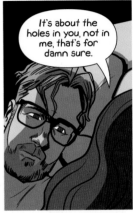

It's about the holes in you, not in me, that's for damn sure.

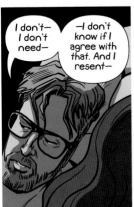

I don't— I don't need—

—I don't know if I agree with that. And I resent—

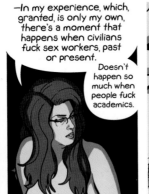

—In my experience, which, granted, is only my own, there's a moment that happens when civilians fuck sex workers, past or present.

Doesn't happen so much when people fuck academics.

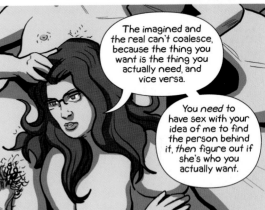

The imagined and the real can't coalesce, because the thing you want is the thing you actually need, and vice versa.

You *need* to have sex with your idea of me to find the person behind it, *then* figure out if she's who you actually want.

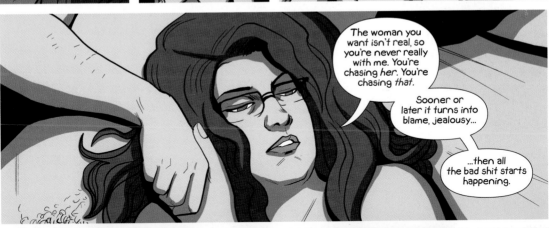

The woman you want isn't real, so you're never really with me. You're chasing *her*. You're chasing *that*.

Sooner or later it turns into blame, jealousy...

...then all the bad shit starts happening.

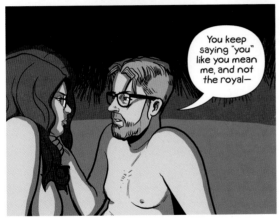

You keep saying "you" like you mean me, and not the royal—

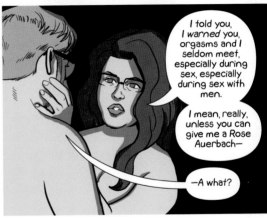

I told you, I *warned* you, orgasms and I seldom meet, especially during sex, especially during sex with men.

I mean, really, unless you can give me a Rose Auerbach—

—A what?

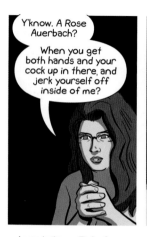

Y'know. A Rose Auerbach?

When you get both hands and your cock up in there, and jerk yourself off inside of me?

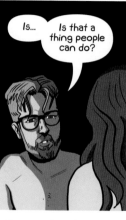

Is... Is that a thing people can do?

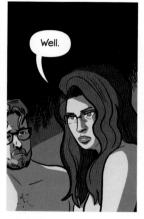

Well.

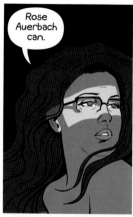

Rose Auerbach can.

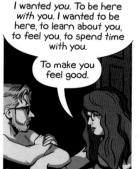

I wanted *you*. To be here with you. I wanted to be an here, to learn about you, to feel you, to spend time with you.

To make you feel good.

You were here to write a sentence with an exclamation point at the end about how... virile you are, how able, how competent.

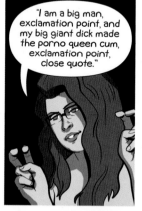

"I am a big man, exclamation point, and my big giant dick made the porno queen cum, exclamation point, close quote."

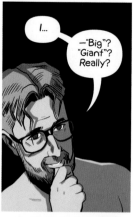

I...

—"Big"? "Giant"? Really?

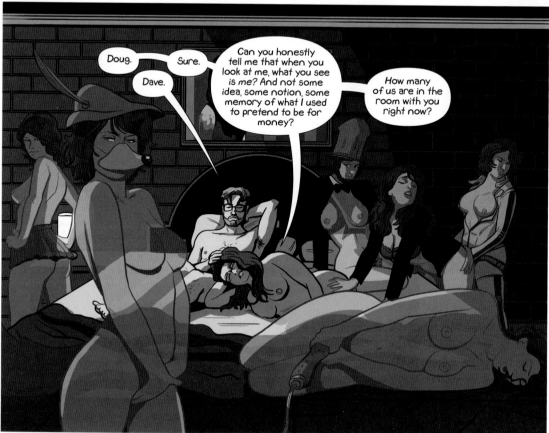

Doug. Sure.

Dave.

Can you honestly tell me that when you look at me, what you see is *me*? And not some idea, some notion, some memory of what I used to pretend to be for money?

How many of us are in the room with you right now?

c'mon.
c'mon.
aaa
Please.
Please ow
ow—
snf
goddammit.
snff
bullshit...
Are you
screening
calls?

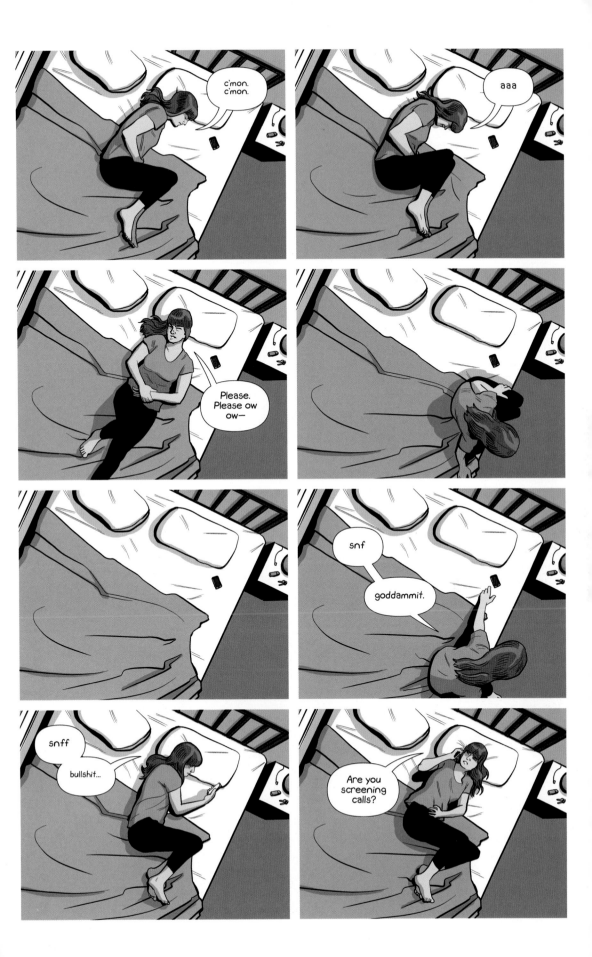

GARY

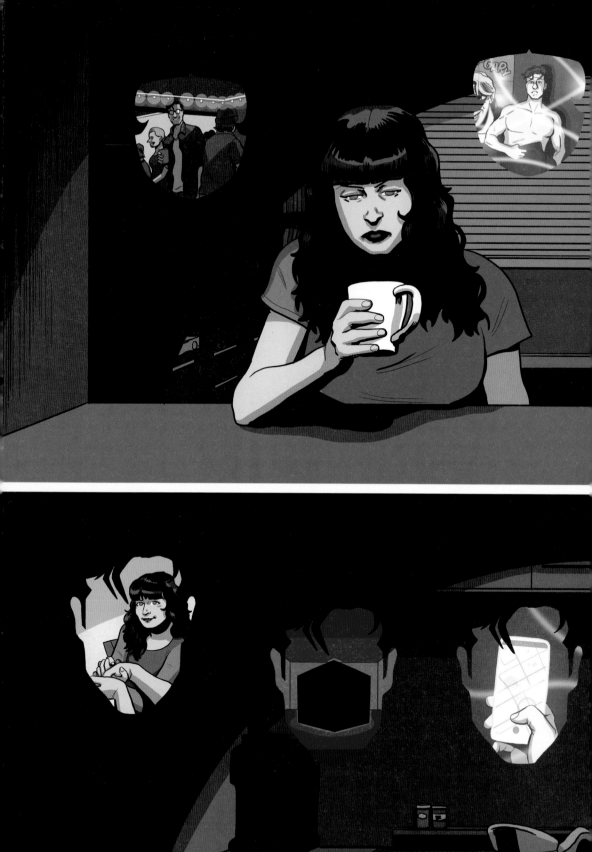

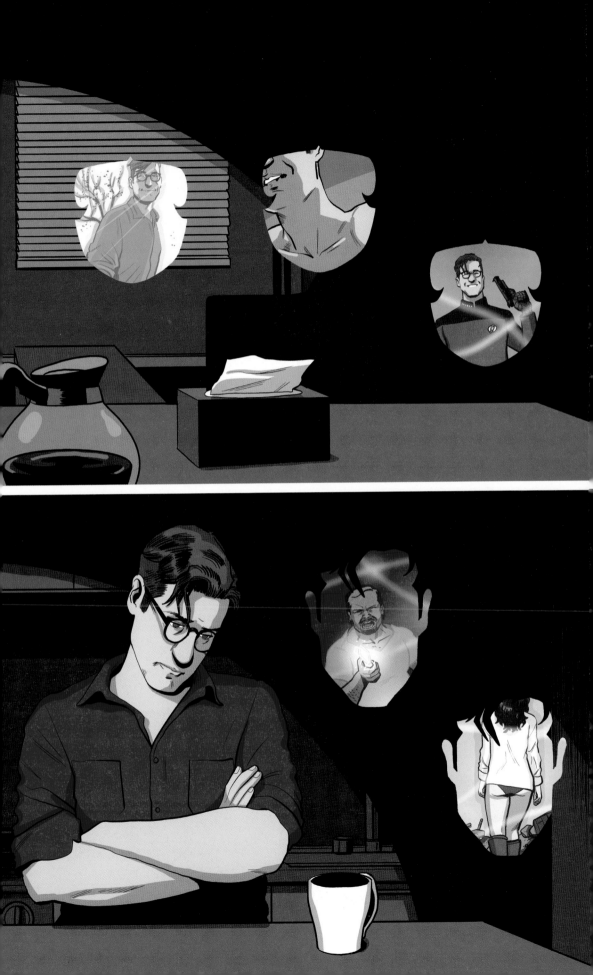

Hey hey—
Maybe this isn't the best idea.
Nope.
robolover
This is totally a bad idea.

But we do it anyway.
One final time.
One for the road.
For everything.
I'm suh—
I'm so sor—
No.
No crying. No apologies.
Then, just like that...
...It was over.

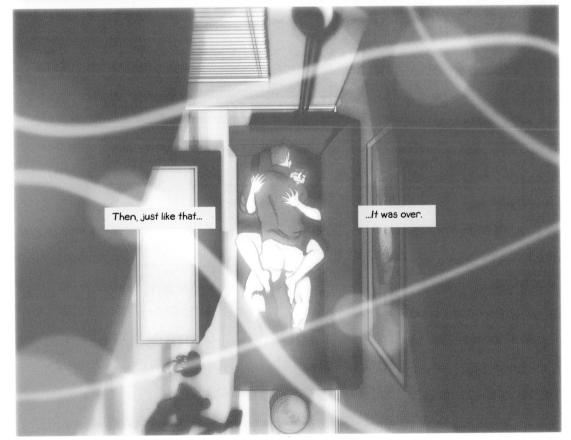

life.

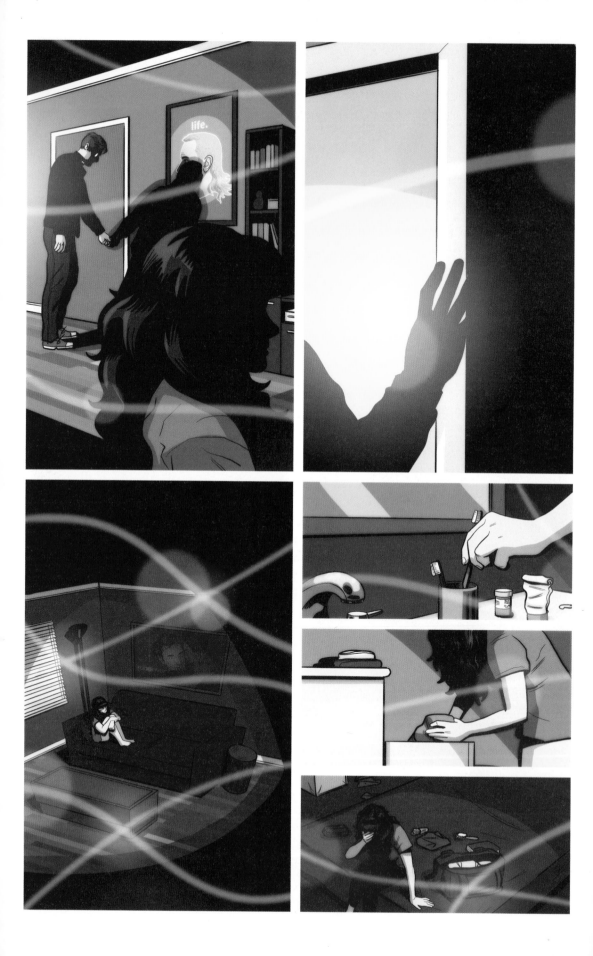

RED CRAB
LA DEE FUCKING DA FRENCH BISTRO
BADALCORP

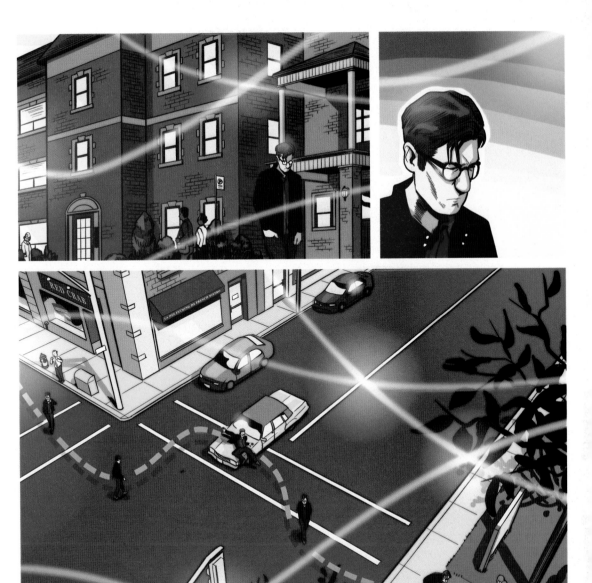

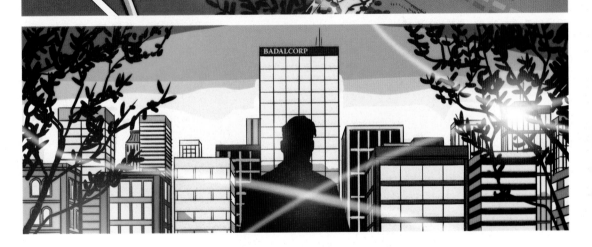

EXIT

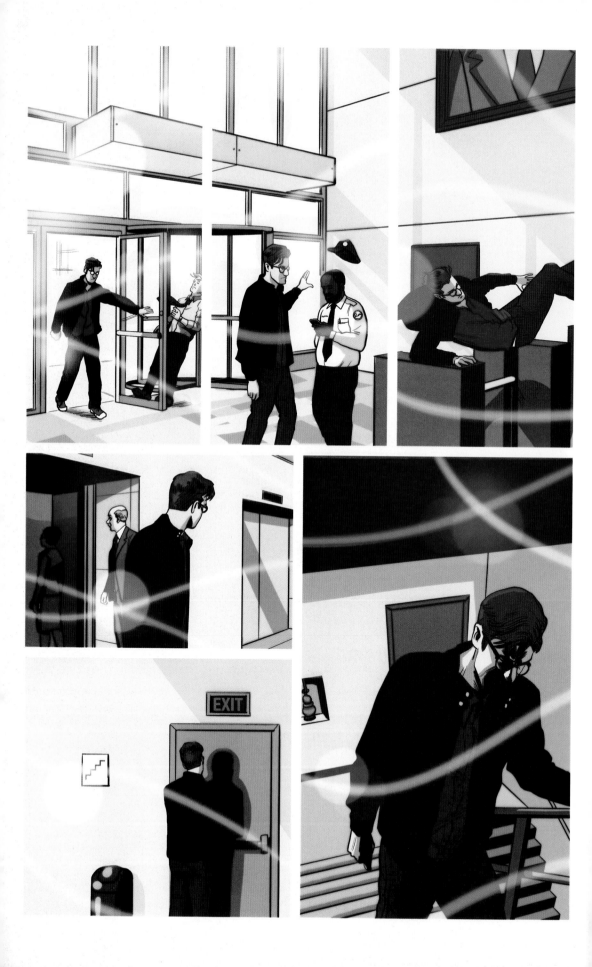

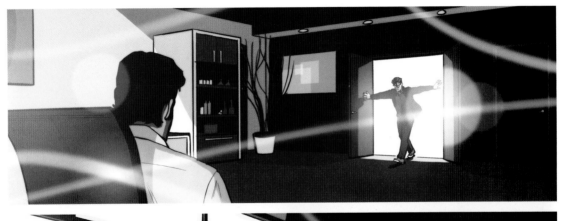

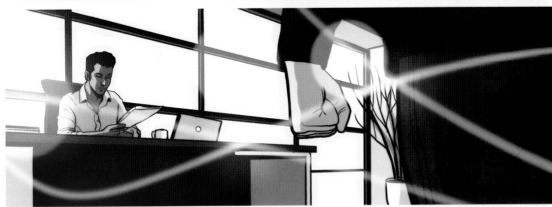

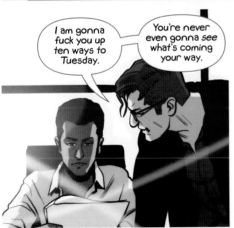

I am gonna fuck you up ten ways to Tuesday.

You're never even gonna *see* what's coming your way.

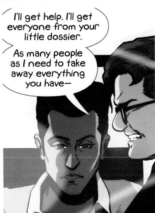

I'll get help. I'll get everyone from your little dossier.

As many people as I need to take away everything you have—

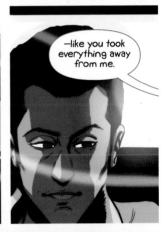

—like you took everything away from me.

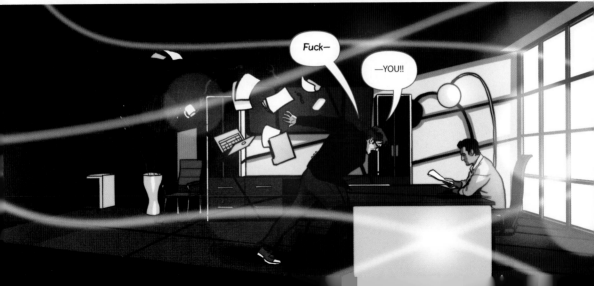

Fuck—

—YOU!!

And fuck this!
And this!
And this!
Fuck YOU!
My oh my.
A challenge.
What the hell is wrong with you?
I didn't say "stop sucking."

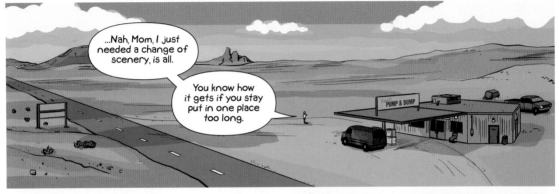

...Nah, Mom, I just needed a change of scenery, is all.

You know how it gets if you stay put in one place too long.

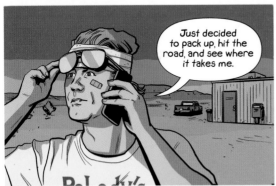

Just decided to pack up, hit the road, and see where it takes me.

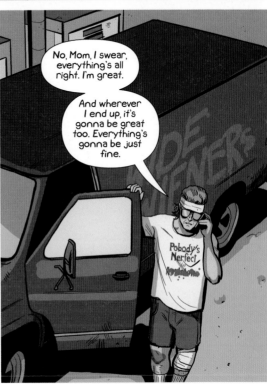

No, Mom, I swear, everything's all right. I'm great.

And wherever I end up, it's gonna be great too. Everything's gonna be just fine.

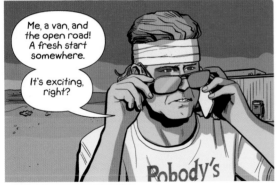

Me, a van, and the open road! A fresh start somewhere.

It's exciting, right?

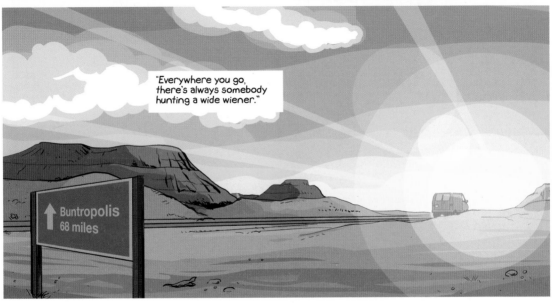

"Everywhere you go, there's always somebody hunting a wide wiener."

↑ Buntropolis
68 miles

I don't know how it happened or why, just.
At some point he started getting meaner and meaner.
He's an asshole. You knew that. I knew that.
I know, I know, I just...
I just, it's so hard for me to find a good boyfriend, let alone one I have this thing in common with.
And I know you told me not to mix work and personal, but it's all tied up together now, and I'm not sure how to—
—Watch it.
RED CRAB
Watch what?
sigh
Doesn't matter.

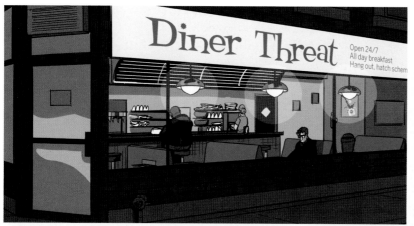

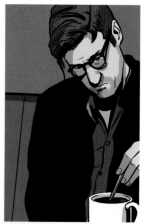

Diner Threat
Open 24/7
All day breakfast
Hang out, hatch schem

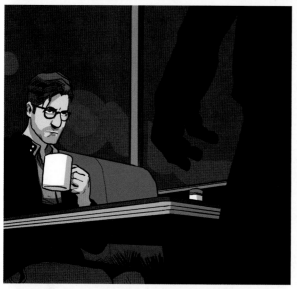

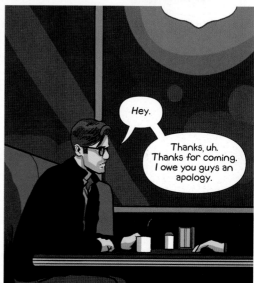

Hey.

Thanks, uh.
Thanks for coming.
I owe you guys an
apology.

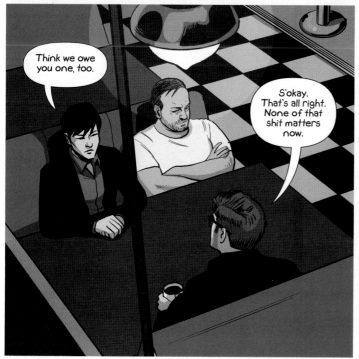

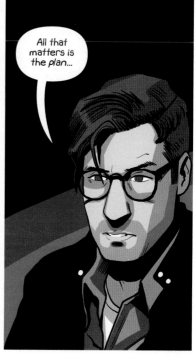

Think we owe
you one, too.

S'okay.
That's all right.
None of that
shit matters
now.

All that
matters is
the plan...

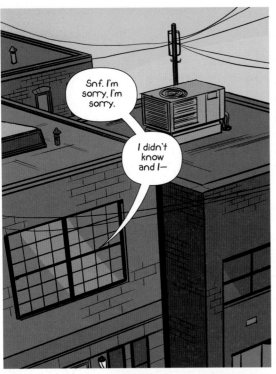

Snf. I'm sorry, I'm sorry.

I didn't know and I—

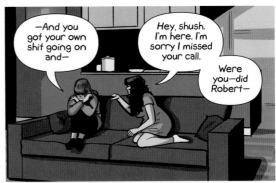

—And you got your own shit going on and—

Hey, shush. I'm here. I'm sorry I missed your call.

Were you—did Robert—

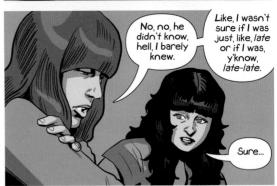

No, no, he didn't know, hell, I barely knew.

Like, I wasn't sure if I was just, like, *late* or if I was, y'know, *late-late*.

Sure...

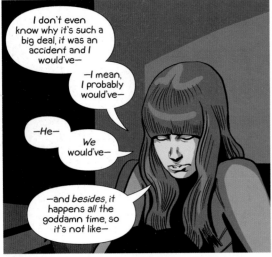

I don't even know why it's such a big deal, it was an accident and I would've—

—I mean, I probably would've—

—He— We would've—

—and *besides*, it happens *all* the goddamn time, so it's not like—

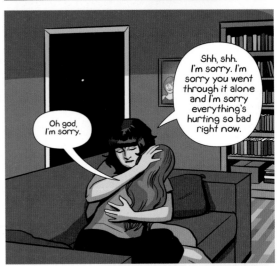

Oh god, I'm sorry.

Shh, shh. I'm sorry. I'm sorry you went through it alone and I'm sorry everything's hurting so bad right now.

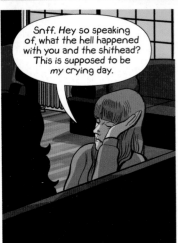

Snff. Hey so speaking of, what the hell happened with you and the shithead? This is supposed to be *my* crying day.

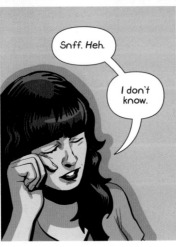

Snff. Heh.

I don't know.

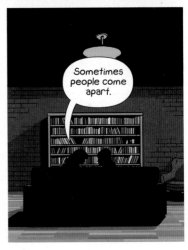

Sometimes people come apart.

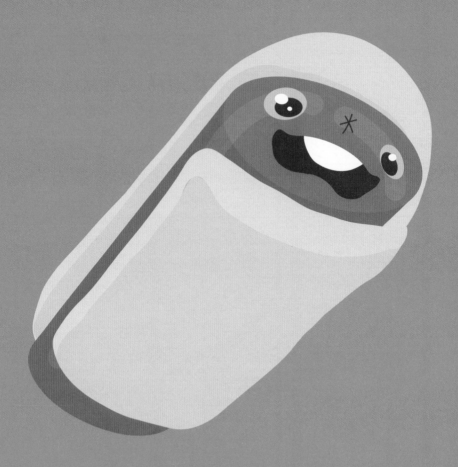

I might be short, but I'm so wide
So wide that I won't fit inside
Just take your time, and gen-tl-y
Soon inside your mouth I'll be

Wide Wieners, Wide Wieners
Stubby, jolly, full of mirth
Wide Wieners, Wide Wieners
I'm not long but I have girth

Wieners aren't one size fits all
Long fat short bent big or small
Just be cool and trust me chum
I'm a wiener

Made for buns

IN THE BACK OF THE VAN WITH THE BLACKED-OUT WINDOWS, THIS IS THE MUSIC THAT PLAYS

The Oral History Of The Wide Wiener Song

Some time during the spring of 2017, two humbly bi-furious comic creators,
Chip Zdarsky *and* ***Matt Fraction,*** *set out to produce the latest issue of their comic book.*
Four days later they returned with the singular greatest creation in the history
of not only comic books, but of America, and maybe even the world probably?

BY ALEX PAPPADEMAS

When *Sex Criminals* premiered in the fall of 2013, few could have predicted that it would become a comic book that would one day see an issue 19 published. It launched one career -- Chip Zdarsky's -- into the stratosphere of mainstream superstardom and ended another -- Matt Fraction's -- in a poof of shame and ignominy. It was the first time a comic book had the word "Sex" and "Criminal" in the title, and the world would never be the same again, which is a thing people said about *Sex Criminals* so enthusiastically and so often

that that guy put it into that song in *Hamilton,* but in that it was about something else and not this, but originally it meant this.

As *Sex Criminals* continued beyond its original conception and began to explore its world and characters, readers became acquainted with several others gifted with (or cursed by) the same "powers" shared by lead characters Suzie and Jon -- the ability to freeze time post-or-gasm. Several of these charac-ters would exhibit variations on that theme: one became a kind of ghost, one became a kind of

monster, and one became…a legend.

A legend with a theme song.

We sat down with several members of the creative teams behind *Sex Criminals* and "The Wide Wiener Song" to talk about their experiences in crafting the jingle that would transform art, mankind, life, love, and the idea of hot dogs as sandwiches -- an intellectual-cum-gastronomic puzzle that still gives us goosebumps all over our boners and gooseboners all over our lady businesses.

MATT FRACTION ("writer"): I think I'd written, or was going to write, that The Little Man was like an ice cream man, but for hot dogs. At that point, (The Little Man) wasn't really a character, so much as an excuse for me to make Chip draw those horrible little sex goblins.

CHIP ZDARSKY ("artist"): I fucking hate those little things.

Fraction: He thinks they're the worst.

Zdarsky: You're the worst. It's why I quit.

Fraction: I think I said he was a hot dog man, and Chip said, "of course, he sells wide wieners." It had to be Chip. I don't know that I'd call them "wieners." I still can't even spell it right. I'd probably say, "Wide Hot Dogs Like Hamburgers But Hot Dog Meat." See, that's not as funny.

Zdarsky:: True story: One day while I was in therapy, my therapist started laughing and told me we should have a character in the book named "Wide Wiener." I asked her to clarify what that meant, but she just kept laughing. So when Little Man needed a job, I knew it had to be selling wide wieners.

Fraction: Like pretty much everything else in the book, without Chip I'd have just gone on to something else and it wouldn't be as good.

Zdarsky: When we did the cover for the solicitation, I showed my therapist the Wide Wiener truck, proudly. She chuckled, and then became sad and quiet. She then whispered, "I shouldn't have told you that." I asked her if she felt she broke some sort of code of ethics and she said no, but that she wanted to maybe write a detective novel some day about a detective named Wide Wiener. I felt pretty bad, but also pretty confused.

Fraction: They used to give us awards for this shit. Can you believe it?

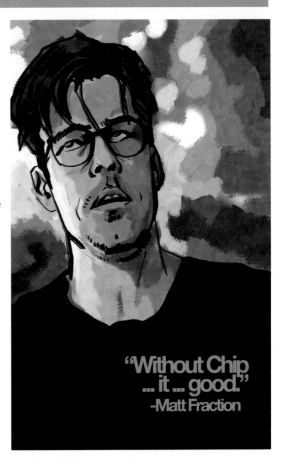

"Without Chip ... it ... good."
-Matt Fraction

Fraction: If he had an ice cream man truck, that'd mean he'd have ice cream man music. Like, a jingle.

JOHN DARNIELLE (musician, author): Matt has no musical talent at all, no.

MIKE DOUGHTY (musician, author): Like -- like none.

JEAN GRAE (musician, actress): He even claps white.

MICHAEL CHABON (author): (Matt) asked me if I could help with the lyrics.

Fraction: I wrote the lyrics first. I think that's how musicers do it? But I don't really understand songs, or lyrics, or rhyming, or meter, or any... anything really. So yeah, of course, I looked up "really good writers" in the Yellow Pages because I live in 1987 and it's from then that I called (Chabon) for help.

Chabon: "Help" isn't the word I'd use, and I have won a Pulitzer Prize for worditry, so I know from good words a lot. I got on the horn with Phil(ip Roth) and Tommy P(ynchon) right away -- this was, like, the emergency triage surgery of "helping." It was like M*A*S*H or something. Just trying to keep this stupid little thing alive before it got shipped off to a better hospital in Pyong-yang.

PHILIP ROTH (author, masturbator): Get off my lawn.

THOMAS PYNCHON (author):

Roth: I'm calling the cops goddammit.

DAVID THOMAS MURRAY (musician, producer, brother of Chip Zdarsky): I'm actually quite an accomplished musician, producer and audio engineer. I play, I don't know, eight or nine different instruments, and spend all day in a ProTools suite, recording and mixing. And Steve (*Chip Zdarsky's false name in the civilian world -- ed.*) isn't too bad a musician either, honestly. But no, no, (Zdarsky or Fraction) never asked.

Zdarsky: He never mentioned a song at all. Just one night... there it was.

KIT COX (Fraction's assistant and office mate): He sat at his desk with a ukulele for like three days and plunked it out, note by note, on these terrible, off-key strings, whisper-singing in this creepy falsetto. In the back of the van with the blacked-out windows, this is the music that plays.

TOM BREVOORT (Editor, Marvel Comics): It sounded like the kind of thing a broken doll would want played at her funeral.

RICHARD M. NIXON (disgraced former president): Literally the music you hear in hell.

Zdarsky: (Matt) sent (me) the song in March of 2017, while I was at a screening of *Logan* with (musician, producer, brother) David Thomas Murray. (So) when I turned (my phone) on afterward, (it) was the first (thing) I saw. It didn't really impact me much initially, because (I was still thinking a lot about *Logan* and the journey the character [of Logan] went on). But eventually (the song) started infiltrating my thoughts about *Logan* to the point where I can no longer separate the two. When (someone) mentions (*Logan*) (to me) now, I (immediately start [singing the lyric {"stubby, jolly, full of mirth,"}]) and that's a testament (to how good the song is, that it's now the soundtrack to *Logan* in my mind).

Murray: The fuck wouldn't they actually get an actual musician? Jesus.

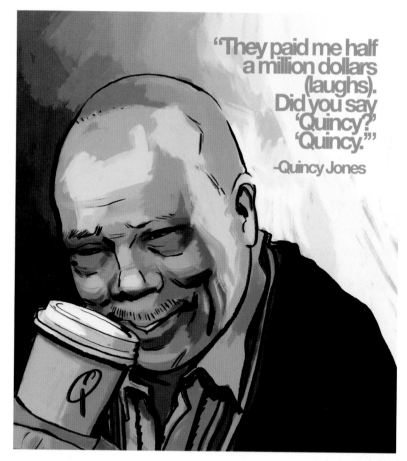

"They paid me half a million dollars (laughs). Did you say "Quincy?" "Quincy.""

-Quincy Jones

3. Upgrading the Upgrade

SETH MEYERS (writer, comedian, talk show host): Hey everybody, welcome to late night, I'm Seth Meyers. We got a great show for you tonight.

ERIC STEPHENSON (Publisher, Image Comics): We knew right away we had something special on our hands, or in our hands, as it were, and wanted to make sure the issue was released with the appropriate fanfare and press attention. We contacted the printers, the distributors, and our retail partners in advance, not just to "prime the pump" as it were, sales-wise, but just to give them a head's up. Something big was coming. Big and wide. Of course nobody could see just HOW girthy a hit like this could be.

QUINCY JONES (music producer, legend): I told Michael (Jackson) when we made *Thriller*, "hey, this is pretty good, you might really be on to something here." Like, deliberately understating things, right? Because it's *Thriller*, it's Michael Jackson, you just knew it was gonna be the biggest thing in the world. But nobody could've seen *Thriller* coming. We thought we knew what the biggest thing in the world was. And while we were right, and it was *Thriller*, what we were mistaken on was either size of the thing or the world. Maybe we thought the world was bigger? So -- so that's it. *Thriller* was as big a hit as we thought it would be, only we thought the entire planet was way larger than it

actually was, so... so it looked bigger than we imagined. But the world got smaller. The record remained exactly the -- like, perspective, right? We needed to see another thing to understand how big the first thing was, or wasn't, but really was because it's like, something very big but it's very far away, or it's something very small and it's very close? Anyway, I'd like a non-fat half-caf mocha, no whip.

Stephenson: We got Q what we were kindly referring to as Matt's "rough demo," and...

Jones: They paid me half a million dollars (laughs). Did you say "Quincy?" "Quincy." Is that the drink for Quincy? Oh, okay. Sorry, it's hard to hear in here.

Stephenson: ...And we let Q be Q and make a hit record. We knew it'd be an upgrade, but Q, he upgraded the upgrade.

ROBERT PLANT (musician, writer): Way way down inside. I'm gonna give you my love. I'm gonna give you my love. I'm gonna give you my love. I wanna whole lot of love. BBBEEEEEERRR-ROOOOOWWWW.

Jones: Yeah, the mocha, no-whip. Yeah.

Fraction: I don't know if Chip ever listened to it.

Zdarsky: We don't really talk any more.

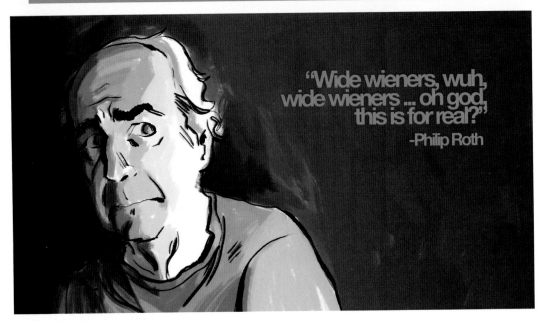

"Wide wieners, wuh, wide wieners ... oh god, this is for real?"
-Philip Roth

Roth: My (muffled audio) Philip Roth. It is April 1st, 2017. I am being well treated by my captors. I have been asked to read (crying) I'm sorry I'm sorry I (muffled audio) (tape break) I am being well treated by my captors. I have been, I have, I have been asked by (pause) (unintelligible) I have been asked by my captors to read the following, uh, the

following message:

I might be short, but I'm so wide so wide that I won't fit inside. Take your, uh, take your time and gen-tl-y, did I say that right? (unintelligible) okay, and gen-tl-y, soon inside your, uh, your mouth I'll be, wide wieners, wuh, wide wieners... oh god, this is for real? Oh god. I (unintelligible) (tape break)

VOICE OF MAN TRYING TO SOUND LIKE PHILIP ROTH WHO CLEARLY IS NOT PHILIP ROTH AND YET IN THE BACKGROUND THE MUFFLED SOUNDS OF PHILIP ROTH WEEPING CAN BE OVERHEARD (hostage taker): Stubby, jolly, full of mirth! Wide Wieners! Wide Wieners! I'm

not long but I have girth! Wieners aren't one size fits all, long fat short bent big or small, just be cool and trust me chum, I'm a wiener made for buns, and also I am the author of *American Pastoral* and *Portnoy's Complaint* and I have read this freely and voluntarily of my own will.

Chabon: (singing): Nailed it.

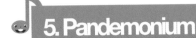

Jones: I loaded up the studio with everyone I ever worked with, wanted to work with, owed a favor, or who owed ME a favor. I wanted a murderer's row of talent. I wanted the new "We Are The World."
I wanted the end of a Rock n' Roll Hall of Fame induction, this isn't -- there's whip. I asked for no whip. No whip. No. No whip. This has whip. If it has whip, how do I know it's actually half-caf? You just want me to trust you? You put whip on and say it's no whip and want me – no, make it again. Start over. Start where I can

see you. Start it over.

HAL BLAINE (legendary drummer, The Wrecking Crew): When Q calls, you come. We got the Wrecking Crew together for one last gig. To play together, all of us, on one last track? I can't think of a better way to go.

CAROL KAYE (bass player, The Wrecking Crew): They called us The Wall of Sound Orchestra, the Clique, the First Call Gang, The Wrecking Crew... we played for everybody. We

played everything.

Fraction: Ooh, did they get Glen Campbell too, or -- oh.

MATT WILSON (Eisner-award winning colorist, THE WICKED + THE DIVINE, et al.): I normally do work in comic books, so it was a little surprising for Quincy Jones to reach out. But, hey, who am I to say no? You want to pay me eight-hundred grand to sit in a recording studio for a week and talk about what colors the walls could be, I'll do it.

Kaye: I think it's safe to say The Crew gave that two-and-a-half-hour recording session all we had to give and then some. It was a very exciting mid-morning for all of us. The old magic was back. And then it was home again in time for lunch and Pilates.

Jones: It's pandemonium in this goddamn Starbucks. Half-caf mocha latte, no whip, come on. It's not rocket science, it's a fucking drink order. Pandemonium. Pandemonium!

Fraction: So they send it to me and they say --

Jones: Put it in the Cloud.

Stephenson: Put it in the Cloud.

Zdarsky: Put it in the Cloud.

Fraction: Put it in the clown? Clown? I don't know what that means. But, okay, now I gotta find a clown.

Zdarsky: Apparently he just, he went out and... you know those guys that paint themselves silver and stand on boxes and pretend to be robots for nickels? Matt goes out, he's got this song on a jump drive, and the first one of these street performers he sees, he just...

Fraction:: He wasn't really a clown, but I thought it was pretty close.

Zdarsky: He just dropped it in the guy's tip jar. And simultaneously grabbed a couple of bucks from it. Later he told me he did that to "keep it legal." I have no idea what that means.

Stephenson: I have literally never heard it. It was the only copy.

Jones: Are you insane? You think Quincy Jones has that kind of data storage just laying around? Hell no, Q keeps his hard drives like a brand new Starbucks: open, clean, and really very small when you look at it. I dumped the track on a thumb drive, cleared off the 44 megs of space it was eating up and got on with my life.

Zdarsky: Apparently it was quite the thing, but nobody ever heard it. Why are you doing an oral history of a thing nobody ever heard, or heard of? That doesn't make any sense. Like, I find your premise to be satirically diffuse. Are you -- what's the joke? The song? The dumb song? Are you making fun of, like, overblown Oral History things that journalists cut and paste together and call it "writing"? Are -- no, no, I'm not mad, I just don't get the joke.

Fraction: I guess in the end, no one did.

.

(Ed. Note - None of the people appearing in the preceding story, including purported author Alex Pappademas, were contacted nor spoken to in any way during the writing of this piece. We just made it all up for funsies.)

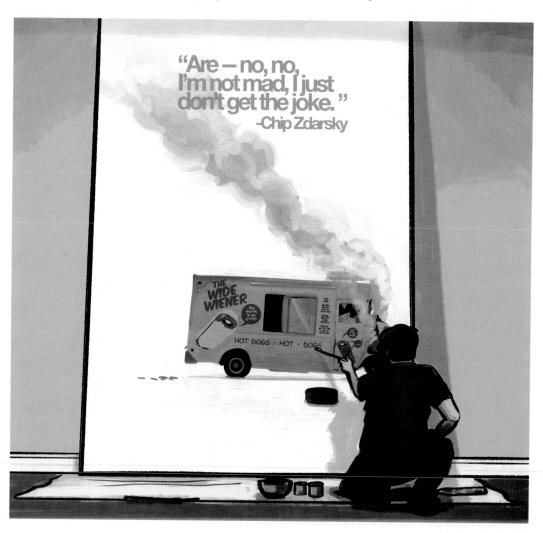

"Are — no, no, I'm not mad, I just don't get the joke." -Chip Zdarsky

Matt Fraction invented the search
engine "Bing" and also using
"Bing" as a verb

Chip Zdarsky has travelled many roads
for many years and it all led him here:
to a bio page reminding you to Bing
him later.

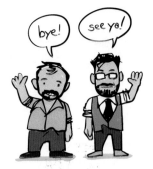